Contents

Commissioning editor: Alan James

Editor: Jan Cumming

Author: Adam Jeanes

Additional research and text: Victoria Burns

Welcome to Arts Council England's guide to the world music industry in England. We hope that you will find this publication both a practical guide, and fuel for thought, as we examine some of the key issues for the sector in the 21st century.

World music has been around in England for several decades – the 1970 Fela Kuti record (see photo opposite) was produced by a British-owned label, EMI Nigeria Ltd. Fela Kuti himself was to be found studying music at Trinity College in London in the early 60s.

At the beginning of the 80s it was possible to count the major world music players on two hands. In the last 20 years the activity has grown exponentially to become a significant and vibrant part of this country's creative industries. The Arts Council has nurtured that activity and helped to build an exciting world music sector in England that is respected globally. This publication describes how it all came about and also provides valuable information for all those involved and interested in the world music industry.

The guide begins with an overview, looking at the current situation of the business and its infrastructure, as many world music operators perceive it to be. These views indicate that the sector has many internal strengths, especially in how it self-regulates the quality of its own repertoire, the professionalism it applies, the value and respect it places on musicians, the commitment it shows in bringing new audiences to different musics and in the productivity of its networking. There are however opportunities for development, such as the extent to which the world music business synchronises and interacts with artists and organisations arising from Britain's own culturally diverse communities. Particularly when, in recent years, many great talents living in our towns and cities have started to appear on prestigious concert stages around the world.

Fela Kuti –
British label release
Photo: Elliot Jack

Support for culturally diverse and diasporic arts is a major part of Arts Council England's work and it is timely therefore, with the first Womex in the UK in 2005, to take stock. This publication does that by tracing the history of world music and providing a wealth of information on musicians and organisations and all those involved in the current business. The overview of the world music scene at the beginning of the guide is based on interviews and desk research. The second part is a directory of organisations arranged by type. The directory is selective and is designed to indicate the range and variety of activities that take place, and give some sense of their inter-connections.

The research focuses on England, but refers to Northern Ireland, Scotland and Wales.

We hope that you will find *world music in England* helpful, whether you are seeking some further context from a British perspective or looking over at our activities from abroad.

Whatever your reasons for using this book we hope you will agree that world music in Britain has made an important and dramatic impact – not just on the way we listen to music but on how we look at life.

Kim Evans, Executive Director, Arts
Alan James, Head of Contemporary Music
Arts Council England

World music: used initially by ethnomusicologists to refer to the diverse local musics of the world, **'world music' has also become a term for any commercially available music of non-Western origin,** and for musics of ethnic minorities; it is also applied to contemporary fusions or collaborations with local 'traditional' or 'roots' musics and Western pop and rock musics.

Oxford Dictionary of Musical Terms, Oxford University Press, 2004

Introduction

In July 2004, the MORI market research agency asked 1,577 English and Welsh public houses, hotels, inns, clubs, student unions, restaurants, cafes, members clubs, churches and community halls what kinds of live music they had presented in the last 12 months. Of those that said they had (47%), 5% said 'world music'.

There are, according to MORI, 151,176 public houses, hotels etc in England and Wales. Mathematics suggests, therefore, that throughout England and Wales between July 2003 and July 2004, there were at least 3,552 world music gigs. And this does not include the hundreds of events held annually in concert halls, theatres or at festivals in England.

Rita Ray and Max Reinhardt from The Shrine
Photo: Carol Sambili

But the accuracy of MORI's findings depends on whether these venue managers happened to have a copy of the *Oxford Dictionary of Musical Terms* or something similar to hand. Almost no other type of music is as difficult to define as 'world music'. There is, as DJ Charlie Gillett has said, 'no rule book' for world music. Perhaps this uncertainty of definition is the reason why world music featured so little in MORI's poll. Other, more definable styles such as jazz and folk scored 20% and 10% respectively.

A similar problem is posed by another recent survey for the *Observer Music Monthly* magazine (July 2005). ICM asked 1,083 Britons over the age of 16 about their music listening and buying habits. When asked what their favourite type of music was, 2% named world music. Unfortunately the interviewers didn't ask '…and what is your next favourite?' Nor is it clear what the interviewees classed as world music. ('Pop', by the way, was the top choice at 27% – a category which is, of course, transparently clear to everyone.)

In Britain, the British Phonographic Industry (BPI) (see Support bodies) which provides annual statistics on record sales, reported in 2003 that world music as a 'genre' accounted for a 0.5% share of the total market sales (up from about 0.4% in the four previous years). But this is hopeless, says Ian Anderson, editor of *fRoots* magazine (see Media: Journals and magazines). 'The world music market must be a substantial part of the record retailers' income – look at how much retail space HMV and Virgin give it in their West End of London outlets – entire floors.' Certainly as much space as jazz and folk, one could add.

There is, as DJ Charlie Gillett has said, **'no rule book'** for world music.

Earliest references to world music

One starting point for a history of the world music sector in England might be found in the life and work of composer Cecil Sharp (1859–1924). From the first years of the 20th century he transcribed or arranged thousands of English morris dances, ballads, and folk pieces (as many as 3,000 by some calculations), and gave concerts and recitals of his discoveries, which generated much Edwardian media coverage. His international fieldwork began in 1915 when he made the first of four trips to America to collect folk music from the Appalachian Mountains. Sharp was not alone in his interest, and the foundations of the folk movement of the early 20th century, which he helped to cement, provided the first framework of concerts and recitals that enabled the earliest 'world music' (in the form of foreign folk music) to find its audience. The interaction between the British folk networks and world music continues to the present day, especially in the festival circuits.

During the mid 20th century, the rise of jazz and blues in Europe and America accustomed western audiences and musicians to certain forms of African, Cuban, Latin and Caribbean music. The stationing of many American troops in Britain during World War II brought these forms right into the heart of English popular culture.

The growth of Western academic attention to music of other cultures led to the creation of 'ethno-musicology' – a word first used in 1950 by Dutch musicologist Jaap Kunst. It was the ethnomusicologists (the hyphen was soon dropped) that seem to have first invented the term 'world music' to describe non-western musical forms – one of the earliest references can be traced to the Wesleyan University,

Middletown, Connecticut around 1953. York was the first UK university to adopt ethnomusicology into its undergraduate and postgraduate teaching programme and the other major UK centres for ethnomusicology are the School of Oriental and African Studies (SOAS), Goldsmiths College and the Universities of Cambridge, Edinburgh and Durham. The Durham Oriental Music Festivals, which were run by the university every three years from 1973 to 1982, were landmark events that raised national awareness of non-western traditional and classical music, alerted larger bodies like the BBC to a potential new audience and served as an inspiration to many world music festivals, including WOMAD (see Festivals: South East).

Influences from abroad and at home

In the aftermath of World War II, the shortage of labour led to the invited influx of peoples from the former British Empire, and created large immigrant communities in places such as Liverpool, Bradford, Leicester and Birmingham with the greatest concentration in the South East and London. This new population brought with it unfamiliar faiths, manners, social structures, attitudes, and, of course, styles of music. The first Notting Hill Carnival was held in 1964 (see Festivals: London). An incredible rise in the popularity of Indian classical music from the mid-1950s onwards began when the concert violinist Yehudi Menuhin championed the music of Ali Akbar Khan and Ravi Shankar in America and the UK: both masters deeply influenced a number of 1960s musicians, including George Harrison. When The Beatles used the sitar for the first time on 'Norwegian Wood' in 1965, it became clear just how wide the boundaries of popular music could be spread. In 1971 the first release on Rolling Stones Records was *Brian Jones presents The Pipes of Pan at Joujouka*.

Throughout the 1960s and 70s there were many examples of mainstream artists adopting non-western music, albeit sometimes as an exotic novelty on cheesy flower-power anthems. English folk music also experienced a boom in the 1970s. (The British folk sector overlaps with the world music scene in England and the author recommends the *Direct Roots* directory [see Media: Books and reference guides] as the best and most detailed publication on that subject.) Andrew Cronshaw, a folk musician who works with many musicians from overseas recalls: 'Exploring your own roots was cool. All things seemed possible – John Peel on the radio was showing how open things could be.'

Because of an increase in racism from the 1960s onwards, successive governments were faced with the question of whether they should reduce racism by promoting assimilation or by promoting multiculturalism. The Labour Government (1974–79) took the latter route, passing the Race Relations Act in 1976 and creating the Commission for Racial Equality. From this point on, socio-political concerns also began to influence UK cultural policy. Bodies such as the Greater London Council actively promoted multicultural arts and music up until its abolition by Margaret Thatcher's Government in the mid-1980s.

In 1985, the Arts Council of England's Music Advisory Panel recommended the creation of two multicultural touring circuits – the Asian Music Circuit (AMC) and the African & Caribbean Music Circuit (ACMC) (see Support bodies) – to assist the nascent network of African, Caribbean and Asian music promoters. In 1986, the Arts Council announced that it was committing 4 per cent of its expenditure to African, Caribbean and Asian arts.

The social turbulence of the 1970s gave rise to a cultural phenomenon which played a big role in the development of the world music sector: punk rock. Punk has had a profound effect on many aspects of British popular culture, and the growth of world music is no exception. As punk began to wane, many of the audience and musicians looked for something else that was not mainstream or overtly commercial. Nigerian King Sunny Ade's *Juju Music*, for example, immediately attracted an audience in 1982 (described as 'worldbeat'). The careers of many world music luminaries began in the punk movement. Joe Strummer (The Clash) formed the world-oriented Mescaleros. Jah Wobble (Public Image) has been working with world musicians of late. Charlie Gillett was once the manager of Ian Dury's Kilburn and the High Roads. And Billy Bragg moved from punk to protest (against Margaret Thatcher) to folk, working with many folk and world musicians along the way, including Eliza Carthy and Ben Mandelson. Radio DJs like Alexis Korner and the late great John Peel (although never fully-fledged world music DJs) had eclectic playlists including a diverse range of African, Latin and Caribbean music. And Andy Kershaw (a former roadie for Billy Bragg) first introduced such bands as the Bhundu Boys on his Sunday night show on BBC Radio 1.

Between 1980 and 1983 there was a period of rapid expansion in world music activity. 'Things seemed to happen very quickly,' Ian Anderson remarks. Hannah Horovitz, who was deputy director of Visiting Arts (see Support bodies) for 18 years, agrees and says that this sudden development should be seen in context. 'There was a growth of interest in international working generally. It was really a case of the UK catching up with the rest of Europe where people had been working across borders for some time. There was a new curiosity about the world's cultures.'

'exploring your own roots was cool.'

Investment in events

Visiting Arts' investments in the early period are a who's who of world music and the organisation gave a whole series of promoters their first 'government' grant. Visiting Arts funded its first African band in 1979 – the Makonde Pop Group from Kenya at the Hammersmith Odeon, followed by the Master Musicians of Joujouka in 1980, and its first officially entitled 'world music' event at the Commonwealth Institute as early as 1981. In 1982 it gave a grant to the first WOMAD (World of Music, Arts and Dance) festival, and continued to give grants to a number of pioneering organisations, including the Music Village (a Commonwealth focus in 1984 and a Caribbean focus in 1986), various WOMAD tours and festivals throughout the 1980s, Indonesian musicians at the Durham Oriental Music Festival in 1982, and Arts Worldwide's UK tour seasons between 1983 and 1987.

Folk festivals also received support for international musicians: the folk festivals of Billingham, Cambridge and Sidmouth made pioneering presentations of music from overseas.

But of all the early events, WOMAD is the most significant. It was created in 1980 by Peter Gabriel, Bob Hooton, Thomas Brooman and others and held its first event in Shepton Mallett in 1982. WOMAD steadily grew throughout the 1980s to become the most significant UK gathering of its kind. In the 1990s, it established itself in its annual Reading site where it has capacity audiences (about 25,000) and there are now a number of WOMAD 'franchises' around the world. Alongside the festival, Gabriel also founded Real World Records to record and distribute the music of the featured artists.

The legend of 'the meeting that invented world music'...

Creating an independent sector

Small, independent record labels also blossomed, such as Stern's, Globestyle, Earthworks, the roots label Cooking Vinyl and World Circuit (see Labels and distributors), and rapidly expanded their catalogues with both original and licensed material. Stern's record shop, in the back of an old electrical store on Tottenham Court Road, London, was the first major outlet for African music in the UK. There were a number of records that broke through to the mainstream at this time: indie label 4AD scored a major hit in the UK with Marcel Cellier's recording *Le Mystere des Voix Bulgares* (1986). But the most prominent mainstream breakthrough came from America: Paul Simon's *Graceland* (Warner Brothers, 1986), which featured Ladysmith Black Mambazo and introduced African music to a wider UK public than ever before.

By the mid-1980s this group of enthusiasts and small organisations had formed a busy but disparate subsector of the music business. Reflecting their diverse origins in punk, folk, ethnomusicology, jazz and so on they had adopted a plethora of terms to describe the music they presented or recorded: worldbeat, ethnobeat, ethnic, international pop, international folk, roots, tropical, and of course, world music, to name but a few.

Billingham International
Folklore Festival programme

Confusion in the sector led to confusion in the record stores. Haphazard cataloguing made it difficult for the increasing number of record buyers to find or browse CDs of international music. Some kind of standardisation was needed. On 29 June 1987 a small group of promoters, festival producers, journalists and record label managers convened a meeting in the Empress of Russia public house in London to see if they could agree on a single overarching name.

The legend of 'the meeting that invented world music' is well known and is detailed in Ian Anderson's article 'World Wars' for his UK magazine *fRoots*; but it is worth retelling.

The meeting was completely practical and had no other agenda other than how CDs should be racked. It certainly was not a philosophical discussion about ethnomusicology. Having compromised on the term 'World Music' as the best description of what they were all presenting, the most significant decision came towards the end of the meeting when each organisation agreed to contribute to the fees of a marketing consultant and to cover the cost of creating CD dividers with 'World Music' printed on them. The *New Musical Express* (NME) (See Media: Journals and magazines) later agreed to carry a compilation cassette of world music on its front cover.

'I know a lot of people in world music, but I go to Womex and there are 2,000 delegates. **Who are all these people?**'

The marketing campaign was a triumphant success. The record shops finally had a convenient category for all these exotic recordings. The music press, after some initial carping – which in many cases still continues to this day – leapt on the concept of world music. A turning point came when the two most influential London listings magazines, *City Limits* and *Time Out*, both adopted the term in their pages. A new genre of music was born overnight. As Ian Anderson writes in his 'World Wars' article the initial world music media campaign in 1987 'bought more column inches and airwave hours pound-for-pound than any other campaign in the history of the music biz'.

One could speculate on what would have happened if the campaign had fallen flat or faltered. Would these competitors have gone on meeting or would they have broken up and gone their separate ways? Or would we now be referring to the Tropical Music sector instead? It is likely they would have stuck at it, because by the time they met at the Empress of Russia in enlightened self-interest, they already had a shared enthusiasm. Most of the people at that meeting are still in world music and, far from being hard-bitten music execs, they still get emotional when they encounter something new and ring all their friends.

It is this 'fan club' atmosphere that is the most obvious characteristic of the world music sector. And in every 'club' there is a committee. During the research for this publication several interviewees humorously referred to a group of individuals who formed the British 'world music mafia'. One interviewee remarked that if you impress 10 key people you will have a certain hit. He then went on to name the 10 individuals, counting them on his fingers (and modestly leaving himself out).

Jaipur Kawa Brass Band, 2005 tour
Photo: Kawa Music

Donna Vose, Arts Projects Manager at Visiting Arts, is in a good position to compare world music to other sectors. 'There is a strong informal UK network,' she says, 'much more developed than in theatre or dance, for example…There seems to be a group of people who trust one another's opinions, and are prepared to take a risk on work they haven't even seen.'

However, a novice coming into the sector may find this off-putting. In order to break in you have to impress and the 'world music mafia' very quickly suss out whether you are out to make a quick buck or are serious about your music. Nevertheless, the sector has grown organically and exponentially since 1987. Katerina Pavlakis (KAPA Productions, see Venues and promoters: London) is not alone when she says, 'I know a lot of people in world music, but I go to Womex and there are 2,000 delegates. Who are all these people?'

Throughout the late 1980s and 1990s, the new sector found its feet spectacularly well. Salif Keita's album *Soro* (1987) on Stern's and Nusrat Fateh Ali Khan's *Musst Musst* (1990) on Real World were two early high points in the new world music market, but there were many others, including the huge success of Fela Kuti. It became an age of collaborations and 'crossover' albums. World Circuit Records encouraged the collaboration of Ry Cooder with Ali Farka Toure, and Youssou N'Dour's crossover album *The Guide: Wommat* (Sony, 1994) scored him an international hit with his duet with Neneh Cherry, 'Seven Seconds'. But the biggest-selling UK world music record of the decade (indeed of all time) was World Circuit's *Buena Vista Social Club* (1997) which has sold (to date) just over 6.5 million copies.

Finding a larger audience

As the 1990s drew to a close a wider range of venues and festivals (big and small) were finding space in their programmes for world, traditional, folk and culturally diverse music. Events at the South Bank Centre and the Barbican in London grew in size and popularity. Across the country there was a steady rise in the number of world music events, most notably in local arts centres. Many of the venue managers currently working in the sector cut their first world music teeth in these arts centres.

The 1990s also saw the growth and increasing professionalism of melas and carnivals (many started out as independent entities and then became the responsibility of local authorities) which drew larger crowds than ever before. In 1997 the National Lottery introduced Arts4Everyone grants and many smaller, culturally diverse community organisations developed music events of their own for the first time. As some culturally diverse communities are in deprived urban areas, geographically-focused economic regeneration schemes see this kind of community-led arts work as a useful tool in their social cohesion work, with music (arguably less elitist and more accessible than drama or literature) playing an important role, especially among refugee and asylum-seeking groups. Organisations like Arts Worldwide (founded by Anne Hunt in the 1980s) had moved from touring to creating larger projects such as their series of cultural festivals of refugee and diaspora communities in the UK (Afghanistan in 1992, Kurdistan in 1993, Horn of Africa 1994 and Armenia 1995). Cultural Co-operation's Music Village (see Festivals: London) received a grant from the Home Office, and the organisation began its mapping of London's Diasporic cultures.

World music (in a modified form) was now being **brought to** an even wider, even **younger audience**.

The rise of club and dance music throughout the 1990s sucked in and sometimes spat out various world musicians whose works were sampled and remixed to the thump of drum machines. 'Global' dance became a thriving sector including a hugely successful remix of Nusrat Fateh Ali Khan by Massive Attack, one of the most influential British groups of the 1990s. World music (in a modified form) was now being brought to an even wider, even younger audience. And although many 'traditionalists' regarded it as the worst kind of commercial 'contamination' of traditional music (especially since the music was not live) the world music touring circuit easily expanded to take in clubs and dance venues, such as The Shrine (promoted by Rita Ray and Max Reinhardt, see Venues and promoters: London) created in the image of Fela Kuti's Lagos venue. Bhangra and Desi Beats also became popular forms.

The advent of the British Asian underground scene, centred around Talvin Singh's club Anokha and west London label Nation records, demonstrated that Asian dance music could compete with anything pumping out of Ibiza's clubs. Asian pop stars like Apache Indian, State of Bengal and Asian Dub Foundation made their first appearance in the UK Pop Charts and the Bollywood 'craze' began. In April 2001, British Foreign Secretary, the late Robin Cook, caused a stir when he said that Chicken Tikka Massala was the 'true British national dish' because it was 'a perfect illustration of the way Britain absorbs and adapts to external influences.' This ability to 'absorb' was certainly true of the British dance music scene as it entered the new millennium.

L to R: Mariza, Rita Ray
and Michael Nyman –
BBC Radio 3 Awards
for World Music, 2003
Photo: James McCauley

World music
and the media

One of the most significant developments in the UK sector in recent years has been the BBC's showcasing of world and culturally diverse music, spearheaded by BBC Radio 3 (see Media: Broadcasting). This predominantly classical music station has developed a portfolio of world music-oriented programmes presented by the likes of Andy Kershaw, Lucy Duran, Verity Sharp and Fiona Talkington (to name only four). The BBC's World On Your Street project and the 2005 season of Africa Lives on the BBC are also seen as positive. But the most high profile of the BBC's commitments has been the creation in 2002 of the Awards for World Music, emulating the highly successful BBC Radio 2 Folk Awards. The Awards are still in their infancy,

but it is already clear that they are influential in promoting world music to larger audiences and in promoting the careers of the award winners themselves. Mariza (winner in 2003) spoke at the 2005 Award ceremony of how much the award had meant to her: 'Something changed when [I] started working again…[the Awards] opened the door to a new audience.' And Audience Award winner Ivo Papasov returned home from the same awards and was snapped up by the Bulgarian Ministry of Culture to appear in a TV advert promoting Bulgaria's tourist industry abroad. 'It is the first time that I am meeting Bulgarian culture minister and I am extremely happy to see such a young person,' he charmingly remarked.

Perhaps a 'World FM'?

Yet the general feeling, in the sector, is that there is not enough airtime (on the BBC and elsewhere) to do world music justice. Some say that broadcasters are biased towards West African music at the expense of music from East Africa. Another frequent comment is that most of the regular world music programmes go out at non-peak times, and *World Routes* in particular was described as 'a bit anthropological and niche' by one interviewee. *Late Junction*'s world music content is disappointingly low, said another. Another felt that Radio 3 approaches its world music output just as it does its classical music output – in the sense that it does not seek to popularise classical music in the way that the independent commercial radio station Classic FM does. Perhaps a 'World FM' might be useful? (It should be added that – in a manner typical of all world music professionals – all these individuals went on to express admiration for their broadcasting colleagues.)

In 2005, the **general public** have a **greater understanding** and knowledge of music from abroad…

The world music sector has always had an uneasy relationship with the UK media. Part of this uneasiness between the sector and the media arises from the way in which it came into being. World music has never disguised the fact that it was invented as a 'trick' played on the music press to get more attention. But that was when the artists themselves were not well known and the audience for world music was small. Now in 2005 many feel that it has simply outlived its usefulness. The general public have a greater understanding and knowledge of music from abroad (especially Africa) and it is time to file world artists back in the hip hop, jazz and pop sections alongside their (supposedly) better known Anglo-American peers. 'The term world music is like a chain around the necks of some artists,' says Ian Ashbridge, director of Wrasse Records (see Labels and distributors). 'It is too easily dismissed by the mass media as "specialist". You cannot lump Daara J, a hip hop crew, Ali Farka Toure, a blues artist, and Rachid Taha, a punk under the same musical category.'

Seckou Keita
Photo: Zule

A 'good seller'

Naturally others express a slightly different view. Yes, the boundaries of world music blur into jazz, folk and even rock, pop and dance, and it is important that artists have the opportunity to cross into those genres, but there is definitely something distinct and definable at the centre which needs to be preserved and be called 'world music'. Paul Fordham of Cactus Jazz and Way Art West (see Agents and managers) identifies this in terms of a kind of 'incubator' for culturally diverse artists. 'World music is a rich source for other musics – particularly for urban and dance. It maintains traditions, musical roots and identity, and inspires culturally diverse awareness in practitioners and the audience.' The British music industry as a whole is a major source of repertoire globally, second only to America. World music plays an important role in supplying new talent: the number of times world musicians are nominated for or win the big UK music prizes testifies to this. Many mainstream artists take inspiration from world music: Damon Albarn (Blur and Gorillaz) and Robert Plant being the most high-profile new converts.

Nevertheless, record sales in the sector are generally low. A 'good seller' in UK world music is around 5,000–10,000 units, although there are, as we have seen, some problems in establishing definitive statistics. Another important aspect is that, unlike pop records, which generally have a short shelf-life, many world music records sell in good numbers over a long period of time: EMI are still selling records by Nusrat Fateh Ali Khan nearly 20 years after they were released. But even if world turns out to be a 'cottage industry' within the UK music business, no one could deny that it contributes to the diversity of the UK's live and recorded music and is a consistent source of new, non-mainstream artists. In fact, if true, this would confirm a feature of world music in the UK: that it has always punched considerably above its weight.

Athena Andreadis
BBC Radio 3
World On Your Street
Photo: Michael Williams

Small is beautiful

With low record sales, live touring is therefore the main income generator in the UK sector, in direct contrast to the Rock and Pop industry, where live work is seen as a promotional activity to sell records. The world music's reliance on earned income from gigs is problematic as fees from the seated venues (where world music is mainly presented) and from UK festivals, are generally lower than in mainland Europe. In many cases, there is little money left over to carry out artist development. Several promoters and agents commented positively on the contribution of Arts Council England in this area. Arts Council England concentrates on live touring and incentivising venues to work in consortia. 'Since the introduction of Grants for National Touring there has been a change in the way tour organisers are able to work' says Alan James, Head of Contemporary Music at the Arts Council's national office. 'Grants for National Touring has enabled some tour producers to act more like curators and artistic directors, generating their own projects. Smaller agencies working with emerging artists, or artists which are 'difficult to sell', can subsidise their touring programmes and strategically develop new markets for their acts.'

'Venues, agents and record labels are **working better** than ever together, whereas big promoters struggle to market this music because they do not have the **cultural diversity awareness**.'

Several of the regional offices of the Arts Council are proactively sponsoring consortia and networking activities to bring people in contact with each other. In the South East, a new world music consortium is being formed. And there are several national consortia which work cross-regionally; most significant of these are Live Roots and Music Beyond the Mainstream (MBM) (see Venues and promoters: National touring consortia). MBM takes in large venues like De Montfort Hall in Leicester, The Sage Gateshead and the Brighton Dome.

Yet some feel that the economic weakness and low fees in the live sector is a bit of a two-fold blessing in disguise: first it keeps the larger entertainment corporations out of the sector along with all the 'distractions' they bring; and second, it draws the motivated enthusiasts (who are doing it for the music) together in order to do justice to the artists they are promoting. Small is, therefore, beautiful, guarantees quality and provides the safe space in which a new artist can develop creatively. David Flower of SASA Music (see Agents and managers) says that it is, again, a cultural diversity issue. 'Venues, agents and record labels are working better than ever together, whereas big promoters struggle to market this music because they do not have the cultural diversity awareness.'

Making an impact

At the same time, the sector is clearly learning the ways of the mainstream. Jason Walsh at Musicians Incorporated (see Agents and managers) refers to the recent Arts Council-funded Africa Soul Rebels UK tour (February 2005) of Tinariwen, Daara J and Rachid Taha. For him it proves that 'it's possible to promote world music in a rock and roll way.' And certainly the tour was very successful. Ian Ashbridge at Wrasse explains the approach: 'The Soul Rebels Tour was marketed in a very specific way and packaged for the media. By not marketing it as world music we attracted a different kind of crowd and a different kind of coverage. The age range was lower. By not having a "niche mentality" we were not in a niche.' The global music culture website Fly (see Media: Websites) agreed: 'This wasn't just the usual world music crowd…Many people in the crowd would normally consider themselves indie/rock fans looking for something a bit different but with attitude…'

So is history repeating itself? Just like the punk rockers came to world music in the 1980s are there a new generation of audiences about to discover it? And is world music ready for it?

Another recent UK event which demonstrated the impact of world music was more controversial. The LIVE 8 event, a series of worldwide 'rock' concerts designed to coincide with the G8 Summit, was announced by Bob Geldof, and instantly faced criticism that a campaign to end poverty in Africa involved no African musicians. In 1985, the original Live Aid event had been criticised for its lack of Black artists, meaning Black British and American stars: in 1985, no one had been particularly bothered by the lack of African artists. But, in 1985, there was no such thing as world music. By 2005, many were astonished and insulted that Bob Geldof and his crew could leave them out. Many said it showed a lack of respect and perpetuated the 'victim' image of Africa.

'By not having a "niche mentality" we were not in a niche.'

Peter Gabriel and the WOMAD team rapidly put together the all-African LIVE 8 Concert 'Africa Calling' at the Eden Project in St Austell, Cornwall. The line-up included many African artists like Thomas Mapfumo who had spent their whole musical lives engaged in political protest, and yet none of them (except Youssou N'Dour) got an opportunity to appear on the main Hyde Park stage. (It also featured a number of UK-based artists such as Chartwell Dutiro.) But the fact that the Eden Project concert could happen at all, and become so controversial, demonstrated yet again how the 'tiny' UK world music sector with its handful of sector operators continues to punch above its weight.

But there was a sad and ironic postscript. LIVE 8 was upstaged just a few days later by the London bombings – terrorist attacks which threw the nation's attention back onto issues which lie at the very heart of world music: **cultural diversity and intercultural communication**.

Ethnomusicology 21st-century style

France is home to a large African community and as a result the popularity of music from Africa is enormous: Malians Amadou and Miriam are megastars of the moment and in Rai (often described as Africa's Rap) there are a string of names who made it big in France: Khaled, Faudel and Rachid Taha.

In the UK the largest ethnic group is Asian (2.3 million, 4% of the total population [ONS 2001 census]) and music from South Asia, if not part of the mainstream, is constantly nibbling at its edges. The BBC Radio 1 primetime show hosted by Bobby Friction and Nihal (see Media: Broadcasting) is a showcase of UK Asian talent. And alongside the dance-oriented work there is a popular growth interest in traditional musics of South Asia. Melas are growing in size and number. There are as many summer schools aimed at Asian youngsters teaching sarod, sitar, tabla and other traditional instruments (like Asian Music Circuit [AMC], and Chakardar in the East of England), as there are music technology courses teaching how to rap, DJ, sample and programme (like Asian Dub Foundation Education [ADFED] and Youth Music Action Zones [YMAZs]). Even on Bobby and Nihal's show, between the 'shout outs' and the 'big ups', there is a remarkable amount of discussion of the traditional origins of the samples on the dance tracks – where does this tune come from? It is ethnomusicology – but not as we know it.

This interest in traditional and classical forms among young British Asians does not surprise Viram Jasani of the Asian Music Circuit (see Support bodies). 'It has always been the case that young people (in the Asian community) are attracted to classical music. It is only now with the increasing number of opportunities that it is becoming clear just how much. And there is simply not enough classical music in the market to satisfy the demand.' The quality is also high among the UK-based professional musicians. The fact that Cultural Co-operation was able to programme a high quality Music Village in 2005 entirely from musicians based in London (of the African, Asian and Middle Eastern diaspora) shows the strength of this indigenous talent.

Bobby and Nihal, BBC Radio 1. Photo: Chris Lopez

Sewing things together

Given the strength of this home-grown 'world' music, it is surprising that there is not more contact between the culturally diverse and world music sectors. Journalist and musician Andrew Cronshaw takes the view that 'There are only a handful of people in the UK world music business and things fall between the gaps. Only a few people are going back and forth sewing things together.' The need to 'sew things together' is becoming more widely acknowledged. Ian Anderson describes the success of Cultural Co-operation's London Diaspora Music Village in 2005 as a 'wake-up call' to the world sector to take note.

In the North West, for example, Eddie Thomas, Arts Council Music Officer in Manchester explains that 'the promotion of world music continues to grow in the programming of the North West venues. To complement this, we have focused on developing the promoters emerging from the Asian and Caribbean communities who are proactively making networks and links between themselves in England and internationally, especially in India and Pakistan.' Investments of this kind in smaller, culturally diverse music promoters are bringing about an interesting change locally, an example of which is the Multi Asian Arts Centre's links with the Alhamra Arts Council, Lahore, Pakistan (see Venues and promoters: North West). Thomas goes on, 'The bigger venues, who five years ago would not have been interested in supporting the smaller organisations in the region, now have a very open attitude, and there are many examples of partnerships, such as the Bridgewater Hall's relationship with Milapfest.'

The Arts Council's resources are highly sought after in contemporary and diverse musics, and there are several issues that the sector faces, which the Arts Council cannot answer on its own. There is some debate among the operators on the overall effectiveness of the various subsidies available to the sector, a lot of which is prioritised on getting the artist into the country and touring rather than on raising the business or fundraising skills of the sector. The UK lacks a central, long-term investment strategy for world music, which would develop the artists, the artforms and the audiences. In the absence of a dedicated fund or national development body, world music finds refreshment at many hands. Regeneration programmes and tourism/ culture schemes by local authorities (they collectively put something like £500 million into the UK arts sector) are one source of funds: many local authorities are the major patrons or organisers of the melas, carnivals and folk music festivals where world musicians are presented. A developmental system like that found in Quebec would be the ideal, say some, which is a mix of distribution (touring), developmental work and partnership building.

UK operators often look jealously at their colleagues in France where state support for artists travelling overseas is a regular aspect of the sector. More support for the practicalities would also be good. The UK visa, work permit and tax position is generally good, in the sense that if an agent or promoter can get the work permits sorted out (for a fee), the visa usually follows. However, the fact that the UK is not part of the Schengen Visa area causes some problems and Visiting Arts reports that it receives more complaints about visa difficulties from overseas musicians than any other group.

…local authorities are the **major patrons** or organisers of the melas…

Current position

In June 2005, the Arts Council published its first International Policy in order to clarify its commitment to the development of international collaboration between English artists and the rest of the world. It is too early to say how this policy may affect the range of international music in England, but it is an opportunity that many presenters and consortia are looking into, and will be something that overseas managers will pick up on. UK agent Rob Challice at Coda (see Agents and managers) says 'I note that a number of international managers are choosing, if they can, to sell an act direct into the UK and bypass using a UK agent. This has been made possible by venue consortia and venues networking at places like Womex. I see this as part of an evolutionary process and on the whole it has to be viewed that it's a positive development that these relationships are happening.

'However it's my opinion that an act cannot sustain a lengthy live career in the UK without using a UK agent that is representing their interests. A non-UK manager can 'cherry pick' one or two festivals or tours in the UK, but unless they are incredibly knowledgeable they will never match the knowledge of a good UK agent/producer.'

Just as there was no 'rule-book' describing what world music was when it was invented so there is no industry strategy describing how it should develop. The LIVE 8 drama underlined the continued marginalisation of world music within the bigger UK music business in an almost textbook collision with the forces of globalisation. The world music sector may have emerged as a moral victor in that clash but its clout was too small to dent Mr Geldof's rollercoaster. The world music sector in Britain has been very good at raising and maintaining production values and promoting internal collaboration, but, as it

…central government should be interested in the long-term contribution the world music sector has made…

currently stands, it is difficult for the sector to understand where it sits in relation to the larger music and creative industries policies of the UK, difficult for it to understand its internal strengths and weaknesses, and difficult for Government to see where and why investment would bring results.

What is needed is an internal self-assessment of the economics, skills and competencies of the sector, and this should be fed into a strategy which enables the sector to present a case for investment to the wider music industry, to public funders and to government.

One could argue that world music is a tiny sector and nobody in power would be very interested. But in fact the music and creative industries as a whole are tiny (despite the rhetoric) compared to say, the British pharmaceutical industry or the weapons industry and yet the level of government intervention in the creative industries is considerable and deliberate mainly because of the spin-off effects they have on the image of the UK abroad and because it represents an area of sustained growth. In addition, central government should be interested in the long-term contribution the world music sector has made to cultural diversity, multiculturalism, inter-faith understanding and to cultural relations between nations over the years.

UK Trade & Investment (see Statutory agencies), the Government's trade agency, openly admits that the music sector is largely unaware of the kind of support it can offer small and medium-sized businesses. Perhaps this is the right moment for a delegation from the world music 'committee' and some of their friends from the folk circuit, the culturally diverse music sector and the club scene, to go and have a talk to the Minister and make some suggestions: like Ivo Papasov, they might be pleasantly surprised by their reception.

Youssou N'Dour
Photo: Véronique Rolland

Directory

Directory key
T: Telephone
F: Facsimile
E: Email
W: Website
C: Contact
D: Date

Information in the directory was
up to date at the time of publication
(October 2005).

Government departments

Department for Culture, Media and Sport (DCMS)
2–4 Cockspur Street
London SW1Y 5DH
T: 44 (0) 20 7211 6200
E: enquiries@culture.gov.uk
W: www.culture.gov.uk

UK government department with responsibility for the National Lottery, and arts and heritage in England only (see also Northern Ireland [DCAL], Scottish Executive [SEED], and Welsh Assembly [CSWL]). DCMS does not directly fund arts and heritage activities but provides funds to a number of 'sponsored bodies' (the 'arm's length' principle), Arts Council England (see Statutory agencies) among them. The DCMS oversees broadcasting throughout the UK, is responsible for the BBC (see Media: Broadcasting), and is the government body overseeing the creative industries including music, in collaboration with the Department of Trade and Industry.

Department for Education and Skills (DfES)
Sanctuary Buildings
Great Smith Street
London SW1P 3BT
T: 44 (0) 870 000 2288
E: info@dfes.gsi.gov.uk
W: www.dfes.gov.uk

UK government department responsible for education at all levels with a public spending budget of just under £30 billion (2004). The Department co-funds Arts Council England's Creative Partnerships programme with the DCMS.

Department of Culture, Arts and Leisure, Northern Ireland (DCAL)
Interpoint
20–24 York Street
Belfast BT15 1AQ
Northern Ireland
T: 44 (0) 28 9025 8825
F: 44 (0) 28 9025 8906
Textphone: 44 (0) 9052 7668
E: dcal@dcalni.gov.uk
W: www.dcalni.gov.uk

DCAL is responsible for arts and creativity, museums, libraries, sport and leisure in Northern Ireland. It funds the Arts Council of Northern Ireland (see Statutory agencies).

Femi Kuti
Photo: Universal France

Department of Trade and Industry (DTI)

1 Victoria Street
London SW1H 0ET
T: 44 (0) 20 7215 5000
E: dti.enquiries@dti.gsi.gov.uk
W: www.dti.gov.uk

The DTI is the government department which deals with the UK's international trade relations, productivity and competitiveness. The creative industries are the fastest growing sector of the UK economy (a growth of 6% per annum 1997–2002, compared with an average of 3% for the whole of the economy over the same period). The DTI's main agency is UK Trade & Investment (see Statutory agencies).

Directorate for Culture, Sport and Welsh Language, Wales (CSWL)

Welsh Assembly Government
Cathays Park
Cardiff CF10 3NQ
Wales
T: 44 (0) 29 2082 5111 (switchboard)
E: CSWL@Wales.gsi.gov.uk
W: www.wales.gov.uk/subiculture/index.htm

CSWL is responsible for administering the Welsh Assembly policy on the arts and culture, Welsh language, National Lottery, libraries, sport, museums, the media and major events (such as the Faenol Festival 2005) in Wales. It funds the Arts Council of Wales (see Statutory agencies) and works with Wales Arts International (see Support bodies).

Farida Parveen in concert,
Arts Worldwide Bangladesh Festival 1999
Photo: S A Sadeque

Foreign & Commonwealth Office (FCO)

King Charles Street
London SW1A 2AH
T: 44 (0) 20 7008 1500 (main switchboard)
T: 44 (0) 870 606 0290 (travel advice)
T: 44 (0) 20 7008 8438 (visa enquiries)
W: www.fco.gov.uk

The British Ministry of Foreign Affairs. The FCO's purpose is 'to work for UK interests in a safe, just and prosperous world'. The FCO champions British arts and culture overseas, and its Public Diplomacy Policy Department (PDPD) funds two major British cultural organisations directly to achieve this: the British Council (see Statutory agencies) and the World Service of the BBC (see Media: Broadcasting). In 2004 they jointly received around £400 million (about a quarter of the total FCO budget). FCO is responsible for the UK Visa Service, which is jointly managed by the Home Office and regulates entry to the UK. (Note: there are several festivals which are exempt from work permits. This list is held by the Home Office and can be found at www.workingintheuk.gov.uk) It also runs a Travel Advisory Service.

Scottish Executive Education Department (SEED)

Victoria Quay
Edinburgh EH6 6QQ
Scotland
T: 44 (0) 131 556 8400
F: 44 (0) 131 244 8240
E: ceu@scotland.gov.uk
W: www.scottishexecutive.gov.uk

The Scottish Executive Education Department is responsible for administering policy on pre-school and school education, children and young people, tourism, culture and sport. It funds the Scottish Arts Council (see Statutory agencies).

Statutory agencies

Arts Council England, national office
14 Great Peter Street
London SW1P 3NQ
T: 44 (0) 845 300 6200 (enquiries)
F: 44 (0) 20 7973 6590
Textphone: 44 (0) 20 7973 6564
E: enquiries@artscouncil.org.uk
W: www.artscouncil.org.uk
C: Alan James, Head of Contemporary Music

The main development agency for the arts in England. The Arts Council is a non-departmental public body (NDPB) or sponsored body operating at 'arm's length' from Government. When the former Arts Council of England merged with the 10 English Regional Arts Boards in 2002, the new organisation was renamed Arts Council England and created one national office and nine regional offices (listed in this section). The national office takes responsibility for the strategic overview while the regional offices are focused on the development of artists and arts companies in their region.

In February 2003, the Arts Council published its *Ambitions for the arts 2003-2006*, a wide-ranging statement on its plans for supporting the arts in England. The funding for these plans is received from the DCMS in two main forms. The first, known as Treasury Funding, is derived from taxation. The second, lottery, is derived from the UK's National Lottery. In addition, the Arts Council manages the Lottery Capital Grant for buildings and renovations (which includes many music

venues). The levels of funding are set every three years in the UK Government's Comprehensive Spending Review. In addition, it offers project funding through its Grants for the arts programme.

The Arts Council's music department covers all genres, from classical ensembles to folk music. The promotion of a culturally diverse music scene is one of the department's main priorities, therefore it supports both international (world) music and English music of an international origin, for example the music of Indian, Asian, Chinese, Caribbean and African artists born or resident in England. It has recently published a Carnival Arts Strategy and its decibel programme is championing the rights of minority ethnic practitioners in the arts.

decibel was an Arts Council England short-term initiative that ran from May 2003 to March 2004 with the long-term aim to support and raise the profile of African, Caribbean and Asian artists in England. (Asian in this context refers to the continent of Asia from Turkey in the West, to Japan in the East.)

It comprised a cross-artform programme of events and projects taking place throughout England. decibel was a moment of change for the arts in this country presenting an opportunity to increase recognition and profile, create stronger networks, and develop managerial skills and artistic talent, in the culturally diverse arts sector.

Chi2, decibel showcase artists. Photo: Huw Morgan

decibel legacy is continuing the work of decibel, ensuring that it remains firm in the Arts Council's commitment to put diversity at the heart of its work.

decibel has organised two showcases (and a third is planned). The 2003 Performing Arts Showcase engaged 81 artists and companies and was attended by over 300 delegates from around the world. The showcase generated £260,500 of touring business for artists. The 2005 Performing Arts Showcase was equally successful, attracting delegates from 16 countries. Both showcases featured a strong music programme.

A third showcase will be held in 2007, in Birmingham. This event will include an international symposium.

Arts Council England, East

Eden House
48–49 Bateman Street
Cambridge CB2 1LR
T: 44 (0) 845 300 6200 (enquiries)
C: Michael Garvey, Music Officer

The East of England has an intriguing mix of rural, agricultural economies surviving alongside world-renowned technological firms (it's been dubbed 'Silicon Fen'). The cultural sector (creative industries, media, heritage and tourism) represents about 6% of the total regional economy. A large number of the population commute to London every day.

The region is prosperous but there are pockets of severe economic depression in the urban areas, particularly Luton, Basildon and Great Yarmouth. Minority ethnic communities make up about 3.2% of the population, with Peterborough home to a large Bengali population and in Luton, a large Pakistani community. Luton hosts the largest annual carnival in England after Notting Hill (see Festivals: East) and a major capital project is planned to create a National Centre for Carnival Arts in the city. The world music circuit in the region is relatively small (the closeness of London often diverts touring) but there are a number of active organisations and many arts centres are presenting good programmes.

Arts Council England, East Midlands

St Nicholas Court
25–27 Castle Gate
Nottingham NG1 7AR
T: 44 (0) 845 300 6200 (enquiries)
C: James Burkmar, Head of Performing Arts and Music Officer

The East Midlands is a predominantly rural area of England, and the majority of the population (just under 4.2 million) live in the Nottingham-Leicester-Derby triangle. The creative and cultural industries in the East Midlands region employ 212,000 people across 25,000 businesses, making up 10% of the total employment in the region. According to recent census data, Black and minority ethnic groups make up approximately 5% of the total population, although this varies widely from 0.3% in the Derbyshire Dales to 28.5% in Leicester. The largest minority ethnic group in the region is British Indian, Leicester has the highest proportion of British Indians in the country. The area is home to a large number of refugees, economic migrants and asylum seekers. Youth Music Action Zones are Corby-Kettering and Lincolnshire.

Arts Council England, London

2 Pear Tree Court
London EC1R ODS
T: 44 (0) 845 300 6200 (enquiries)
C: Philip Butterworth

London is currently the only UK region with an elected regional assembly – the Greater London Assembly, which has responsibility for the arts, culture and creative industries of the capital. London is a major world economic centre: the London Stock Exchange gross turnover in 2005 was £260 million – the third largest in the world.

Of the population of 7.2 million, 1 in 3 Londoners are from a minority ethnic community speaking some 300 languages and representing almost half the UK's total Black and minority ethnic population. Some estimates say that 330,000 refugees and asylum seekers also reside in the capital, mainly of Eastern European, Kurdish or North African origin. Many more are 'invisible' in the official statistics. This demographic mix is reflected in the vibrant cultural life of the city.

Local government in London consists of 32 boroughs and the Corporation of London that looks after the City – all are active in arts and culture and many present their own melas, carnivals and festivals. Any listing of international music organisations in London can only be selective as the city is bristling with festivals and events. Highlights of the year would be the Notting Hill Carnival, Cultural Co-operation's Music Villages, the ongoing presentations at the South Bank Centre and the Barbican, London International Jazz Festival and venues such as The Spitz. In July 2005, London was awarded the 2012 Olympics, which will take place in the extremely deprived East End. As part of the celebrations and to accompany the Games there are plans for an extensive cultural programme that will represent a showcasing opportunity for British and international arts.

Arts Council England, North East

Central Square
Forth Street
Newcastle upon Tyne NE1 3PJ
T: 44 (0) 845 300 6200 (enquiries)
C: Mark Monument, Performing Arts Officer

The North East is the smallest of the English regions with a population of about 2.5 million but has the fastest growth rate in the creative industries (14.4% for 1997–2000). Like Glasgow before them, Newcastle and Gateshead (the region's main cities, which face each other across the River Tyne) have revolutionised their economy and image in recent years through huge investment in culture and the arts. Regeneration projects involving culture, arts and the creative industries are numerous, the most significant of which are sculptor Antony Gormley's enormous *Angel of the North* and the redevelopment of Gateshead Quays, which is home to The Sage Gateshead (see Venues and promoters: North East), the Baltic Centre for Contemporary Art and the tilting Millennium Bridge.

Folk has a major network in the region (especially Northumbrian music) and there are a number of big festivals, as well as a strong tradition of brass bands and wind bands. The regional Arts Centres such as Darlington, Queens Hall in Hexham, the Arc in Stockton-on-Tees, The Maltings in Berwick, and Alnwick, are presenters of world music acts and tend to work in collaboration. The region has a relatively low number of culturally diverse communities (about

2%) but there are a number of small organisations that are actively presenting foreign artists.

Arts Council England, North East is engaged in a number of international projects including Womex 2005, and in 2006 it will play host to the International Federation of Arts Councils and Cultural Agencies (IFACCA) Third World Summit, focusing on arts and regeneration.

Arts Council England, North West
Manchester House
22 Bridge Street
Manchester M3 3AB
T: 44 (0) 845 300 6200 (enquiries)
C: Eddie Thomas, Music Officer

The North West has a population of about 6.7 million. With the legendary music scenes of Manchester and Liverpool, music plays an important role in the cultural life and image of the region.

Liverpool has always been an internationally diverse city, with its shipping industry and trade links. After a period of decline, investment in the creative industries is building Liverpool into a creative powerhouse. The Liverpool Biennale, currently the only international visual arts biennial in the UK, includes international music and performance as part of its programme. Liverpool will also be European Capital of Culture 2008 (with Stavanger, Norway). Manchester is home to the largest UK Chinese community outside London, and organisations such as the Chinese Art Centre (see Support bodies) produce a number of traditional Chinese and fusion-based concerts during the year.

Arts Council England, South East
Sovereign House
Church Street
Brighton BN1 1RA
T: 44 (0) 845 300 6200 (enquiries)
C: Penny King, Performing Arts Officer, Music

The South East is the closest English region to mainland Europe and is home to three international airports with two of them, Heathrow and Gatwick, accounting for over half of the international air travellers through the UK. It has the largest GDP outside London – 15.8% of the UK's total. However, this prosperity is not shared across the region: Kent and East Sussex suffer from high levels of local deprivation. The South East also has a significant transient population of refugee and asylum seekers, many of whom take permanent residence later.

The creative, cultural and sport sectors are an important contributor to the economic prosperity of the region as a whole employing approximately 560,000 and generating a turnover of £46.5 billion.

Despite being densely populated with just over 8 million residents, and home to seven cities with populations of over 100,000, the region lacks a single dominant urban centre and is predominantly rural. Culturally diverse arts activity is largely focused in the urban areas. WOMAD (see Festivals: South East) is presented in Reading.

As the South East is physically close to France (and the Channel Tunnel comes ashore at Dover) the Arts Council has been developing relationships with French promoters and agents. One recent project was Beyond the Sea (Outremer), a partnership between the South East regional office, the French Institute in the UK and Visiting Arts (see Support boddies), which took producers and promoters from the South East and France to ZIFF in Zanzibar. Youth Music Action Zones are Thanet, Slough, Portsmouth and South East Hampshire.

Arts Council England, South West
Bradninch Place
Gandy Street
Exeter EX4 3LS
T: 44 (0) 845 300 6200 (enquiries)
C: Moragh Brooksbank, Arts and Development Officer (Music)

The South West is geographically the largest region of England and the population of around 4.9 million has, since 1981, experienced the fastest growth. Over half the population lives in rural areas and there are significant pockets of deprivation in Bristol, Plymouth, Torbay, Gloucester and Bournemouth. Because of its size, it is extremely heterogeneous and there are many sub-regions. The northern area (Bristol, Bath and Swindon) is more culturally diverse than the south (see The Swindon Mela in Festivals: South West). The region is mainly rural with about 80% of the land in agricultural use. Tourism and culture are two important industries, and the cultural and creative sector employs around 160,000 people, some 7.1% of the region's jobs.

Two significant cultural landmarks are Dartington Hall, which is a centre for musical excellence and teaching, and the Eden Project in St Austell, which presents many musical projects (see Venues and promoters: South West for information on both places). The South West is also home to the biggest outdoor music event in Britain, the Glastonbury Festival (see Festivals: South West).

Music is also an important part of life for two cities in close proximity – Bristol has a vibrant, multicultural music scene and the Bath International Music Festival and the Bath Fringe Festival (see Festivals: South West) regularly present world music, jazz and classical artists. In Cornwall and Devon, indigenous Celtic music and dance are popular.

The fact that the region is a peninsula presents several challenges in terms of touring. There are a relatively small number of promoters and organisations, and most are working with several different artforms and a variety of genres of music at once. But there is no shortage of talent: there are a large number of musicians and studios and Arts Council England, South West receives more grant applications than any other region outside London.

Arts Council England, West Midlands

82 Granville Street
Birmingham B1 2LH
T: 44 (0) 845 300 6200 (enquiries)
C: Andrew Miller, Music Officer

The West Midlands lies at the heart of England. The population of 5.3 million people is mainly concentrated in Birmingham and Stoke-on-Trent. However, over 2 million live in the rural counties (Shropshire, Herefordshire, Staffordshire, Worcestershire, and Warwickshire). Historically, its urban areas have been internationally famous for manufacturing a wide variety of products. North Staffordshire is the centre of UK ceramics, Birmingham has long been known as the city of a thousand trades, Coventry grew with the vehicle, cycle and aircraft industries, and the Black Country towns of Wolverhampton, Walsall and Dudley were the focus of metal production and fabrication. Restructuring of those industries has reduced the number of people working in the sector, but the West Midlands is still the UK's main manufacturing centre.

Demographically nearly 14% of the region's population are from Black, Asian or other non-white ethnic communities. The largest ethnic communities, centred on Birmingham, Coventry, Sandwell and Wolverhampton, are the British Pakistani, Indian and Bangladeshi (representing 7% of the total population). Youth Music Action Zones are based in Birmingham, Shropshire and Herefordshire, Staffordshire and Stoke-on-Trent.

Arts Council England, Yorkshire

21 Bond Street
Dewsbury
West Yorkshire WF13 1AX
T: 44 (0) 845 300 6200 (enquiries)
C: Andrew Herbert, Music Officer

Yorkshire and Humber has a population of nearly 5 million with 44% living in the urban areas of West Yorkshire. Yorkshire has always had a very strong cultural identity, stretching right back to Viking times over a millennium ago. Key industries include engineering, information technology, biotechnology and food, chemicals, healthcare and tourism. Tourism is the region's largest and fastest growing industry providing 5% of the region's GDP. Leeds has become England's largest financial and legal centre outside London while Hull has been dependent on international trade for at least 800 years and has a long tradition of trading with Scandinavian, Baltic and European port cities. The northern area and coast (Scarborough) are suffering from some economic deprivation.

Around 6% of the region's population belongs to a minority ethnic group. The largest minority ethnic group in the region is British Pakistani, living mainly in Bradford and other parts of West Yorkshire. Some of this community is extremely long-established (over 100 years). Sheffield has a large population of asylum seekers and York is home to a substantial Chinese population – the National Centre for Early Music (see Support bodies) presents a Chinese New Year festival.

The Soweto String Quartet
Photo: Hutt Russell Productions Ltd

Arts Council of Northern Ireland
77 Malone Road
Belfast BT9 6AQ
Northern Ireland
T: 44 (28) 9038 5200
F: 44 (28) 9066 1715
E: info@artscouncil-ni.org
W: www.artscouncil-ni.org

The Arts Council of Northern Ireland is the lead development agency for the arts in Northern Ireland and is an arm's length agency of the Department of Culture, Arts and Leisure (see Government departments). It also distributes National Lottery funds in Northern Ireland, received from the Department for Culture, Media and Sport. In collaboration with An Chomhairle Ealaíon/Arts Council (Eire) and the British Council Belfast it runs the international Infodesk, which is an enquiry service based in both Belfast and Dublin with constantly-updated international arts contacts.

Arts Council of Wales (ACW)
Celfyddydau Cymru
9 Museum Place
Cardiff CF10 3NX
Wales
T: 44 (0) 29 20 376500
F: 44 (0) 29 20 221447
Minicom: 44 (0) 29 20 390027
W: www.artswales.org

The Arts Council of Wales is responsible for funding and developing the arts in Wales and is an arm's length body of the Welsh National Assembly (known as an Assembly Sponsored Public Body or ASPB). It also distributes National Lottery funding in Wales on behalf of the Department for Culture, Media and Sport (see Government departments). It funds and works in partnership with Wales Arts International (see Support bodies) on international collaborations and exchanges.

British Council
10 Spring Gardens
London SW1A 2BN
T: 44 (0) 20 7930 8466
F: 44 (0) 20 7389 6347
T: 44 (0) 161 957 7755 (Information Centre)
F: 44 (0) 161 957 7762 (Information Centre)
Minicom: 44 (0) 161 957 7188
E: general.enquiries@britishcouncil.org
W: www.britishcouncil.org

The British Council, founded in 1934 as the UK's international organisation for educational opportunities and cultural relations, is now a non-departmental public body, and is funded by the Foreign & Commonwealth Office with a budget of around £170 million (2004). The British Council is primarily a public diplomacy agency, and although politically independent of British foreign policy, its priorities are closely aligned to current UK geopolitical concerns (Muslim cultures, Africa, EU expansion, the neighbouring countries of the EU, etc).

Its work spans the arts, education, science, governance and English language teaching and examinations through the offices it has in England, Wales, Scotland and Northern Ireland and in about 100 countries worldwide. The Arts, Science and Creative Industries Department consists of about 100 staff in the UK, with local managers in most of the overseas offices. The arts programme presents a cutting-edge, culturally diverse and creative image of Britain, and the department's priorities are collaborations (around 40% of their activity), work aimed at young audiences, arts and social issues and the creative industries. The arts work of the British Council is some of the agency's most public and widely-praised. That said the central arts budget of the British Council is only around £8–9 million, and every year the Council raises around three times that amount from external funding sources at home and abroad.

The arts department works closely with a wide range of partners. Apart from special events, such as the Edinburgh Festival Drama Showcase and Literature Festival Bookcase, the British Council does not fund arts events in the UK (see Visiting Arts, Support bodies).

The Music Department funds a number of touring music projects each year and works with all musical genres (including electronic and club-based music, soul, hip hop and UK garage, classical, opera, music theatre and vocal, jazz, alternative music [guitar-based], roots [incorporating Asian fusion and reggae] and traditional and folk music).

A group of music sector experts from every genre, the British Council Music Advisory Network, provide feedback to assist the department in its policy and work, which has various outlets. The department publishes *New Routes* magazine, featuring articles on festivals, venues, artists and new trends (downloadable from the British Council website). The *Selector* radio show, launched by the music department in 2001 to showcase new British musical talent, won the 2005 Sony Gold Award for best weekly radio programme. (The *Selector* is available over the internet at www.selector-radio.com). With the PRS Foundation for New Music (see Support bodies), the British Council is funding the 2005 Off-Womex stage in Gateshead.

British Library Sound Archive
96 Euston Road
London NW1 2DB
T: 44 (0) 20 7412 7676
F: 44 (0) 20 7412 7441
E: sound-archive@bl.uk
W: www.bl.uk/collections/sound-archive/nsa.html

Founded in 1955 as the British Institute of Recorded Sound, the Archive (sometimes called the National Sound Archive) became part of the British Library in 1983. It holds over a million recordings on disc, tapes and other media. The World and Traditional Music Collection, which is part of the British Library Sound Archive, is one of the largest ethnomusicology archives in the world, and includes published and unpublished works and many field recordings, some dating from the 19th century. The Archive also initiates recording projects and welcomes submissions. Its website contains a set of useful links to other ethnomusicology and world music resources and archives, and its catalogue can be searched online.

Scottish Arts Council (SAC)
12 Manor Place
Edinburgh EH3 7DD
Scotland
T: 44 (0) 131 226 6051
F: 44 (0) 131 225 9833
E: help.desk@scottisharts.org.uk
W: www.scottisharts.org.uk

The Scottish Arts Council supports and develops the arts in Scotland. It is an executive non-departmental public body and is one of the main channels for government funding for the arts in Scotland, receiving its funding (known as 'voted' funds) from SEED (see Government departments). It also distributes National Lottery funds in Scotland, received from DCMS. It is governed by a council, the chair of which is appointed by the Scottish Executive. In the financial year 2004/05, its total budgeted expenditure is £67.5 million (£20 million of which is lottery funding).

UK Trade & Investment (UKTI)
Kingsgate House
66–74 Victoria St
London SW1E 6SW
T: 44 (0) 20 7215 8000
F: 44 (0) 20 7828 1281
W: www.uktradeinvest.gov.uk/ukti/appmanager/ukti/home

UKTI is the government organisation that supports companies in the UK that trade internationally, as well as overseas enterprises seeking to locate or trade in the UK. It is funded by the Department of Trade and Industry.

The DCMS (see Government departments) has responsibility for the UK creative industries (including all genres of music), and works in partnership with UKTI on the international trade aspects. Music falls into the remit of the Performing Arts International Development committee (see Support bodies). In terms of all music sectors, priority markets include the USA, Japan, India and China, where, in May 2005 UK Trade & Investment and the Association of Independent Music (see Support bodies) opened a UK music office in Beijing.

Festivals by English region

East

Cambridge Folk Festival
Cambridge City Council Arts and Entertainment
The Guildhall
Cambridge CB2 3QJ
T: 44 (0) 1223 457 000
E: folkfest@cambridge.gov.uk
W: www.cambridgefolkfestival.co.uk
D: Annual, July, four days

The Cambridge Folk Festival was created in 1964 and is now promoted by the Cambridge City Council. It presents bluegrass, gospel, cajun, zydeco, jazz, world, klezmer and a ceilidh. Recent artists include the Black Umfolosi 5, Tinariwen, the Blind Boys of Alabama and Xosé Manuel Budiño. The festival is broadcast on Radio 2 and BBC Four (TV).

Luton Carnival
Luton Carnival Arts Development Trust
65–67 Bute St
Luton LU1 2EY
T: 44 (0) 1582 876084
F: 44 (0 1582 876084
E: info@lcadt.com
W: www.lcadt.com
D: Annual, May Bank Holiday

The first official Luton Carnival took place in 1976, and it is now the largest UK carnival after Notting Hill (it is the largest one day event of its kind in Europe) and attracted an audience of 150,000 in 2005. The Trust was created in 1998 and is now developing a dedicated national centre for training in carnival arts (with National Lottery capital funding of £3 million). Mainly local artists are presented in a wide range of music: Afro-Caribbean, Urban, Punjabi, Reggae, Irish rock, Garage, Indie, Metal and Hip Hop. It also runs year-round training, education and outreach activities to promote carnival arts.

Norfolk and Norwich Festival
Festival Office
42– 58 St George's Street
Norwich NR3 1AB
T: 44 (0) 1603 614921
F: 44 (0) 1603 632303
E: info@n-joy.org.uk
W: www.n-joy.org.uk
C: Jonathan Holloway, Festival Director
D: Annual, May, 10 days

International arts festival with a programme spanning music, dance, poetry and performance. Previous artists presented include Malia, Hermeto Pascoal and Jan Garbarek.

Anindo Chaterjee performing for Chakardar
Photo: Omkar Chana

Rhythms of the World
PO Box 121
Hitchin
Hertfordshire SG5 2WB
T: 44 (0) 1462 454649
W: www.rhythmsoftheworld.com
C: Bob Mardon
D: Annual, July, weekend

A free street festival with a large international music programme. Previous artists have included Ayub Ogada, Motimba, Ifang Bondi, Yat-Kha and Salsa Celtica.

Southend International Jazz Festival
Southend Borough Council
Cliffs Pavilion Theatre
Station Road
Westcliff-on-Sea
Essex SSO 7RA
T: 44 (0) 1702 331852
F: 44 (0) 1702 391573
E: chasm@cliffspavillion.co.uk
W: www.thecliffspavilion.co.uk

Beginning in 2002, the festival is promoted by Southend Borough Council. Previous world jazz artists have included Surinder Sandhu, Gilad Atzmon and British stars such as Soweto Kinch.

East Midlands

Leicester Belgrave Mela
c/o Belgrave Neighbourhood Centre
Rothley Street
Leicester LE4 6LF
T: 44 (0) 116 222 1905
W: www.leicester-mela.co.uk
D: Annual, July, two days

The Leicester Belgrave Mela first began in 1983 and is one of the longest running. In 2005 it took place at Abbey Park attracting over 100,000 attendees.

Nottingham Mela
Apna Arts
The Art Exchange Gallery
39 Gregory Boulevard
Hyson Green
Nottingham NG7 6BE
T: 44 (0) 115 942 2479
E: info@apnaarts.org.uk
W: www.apnaarts.org.uk

Nottingham Mela is organised by Apna Arts and Nottingham Asian Arts Council (see Venues and promoters: East Midlands) and features local and international acts. The 2005 mela line-up included Rizwan-Muazzam Qawwali, Bikram Ghosh and a showcase of British Asian talent presented by DesiTv.co.uk.

Nottingham One World: One City

Nottingham City Council
The Guildhall
South Sherwood Street
Nottingham NG1 4BT
T: 44 (0) 115 915 5555
W: www.nottinghamcity.gov.uk
D: Annual, May, four days

Taking place in the Old Market Square of Nottingham, this four-day free festival offers music and dance from around the world performed by international and local artists. The 2005 event included Japanese taiko drumming, Brazilian dance, Caribbean steel pan music, African music, Hungarian folk dance, carnival dance, Afghani music, Scottish traditional dance, bhangra dance, dhol drumming and Indian music from the Rhythms of Shakti.

Summer Sundae

De Montfort Hall
Granville Road
Leicester LE1 7RU
T: 44 (0) 116 233 3113
F: 44 (0) 116 233 3182
E: dmh.office@leicester.gov.uk
W: www.demontforthall.co.uk
D: Annual, August, two days

Music festival held at De Montfort Hall, featuring established and rising stars from the UK and abroad. The 2005 festival featured Norwegian Sondre Lerche, Patti Smith and Bellowhead.

Three Cities Create and Connect

Artreach
LCB Depot
31 Rutland Street
Leicester LE1 1RE
T: 44 (0) 116 261 6882
E: threecities@artreach.biz
W: www.threecitiescreate.org.uk

Three Cities Create and Connect, managed by Artreach, celebrates the exciting arts activities, festivals and cultural quarters of Derby, Leicester and Nottingham. Funded by the Urban Cultural Programme, Arts Council and the three local authorities of Derby, Leicester and Nottingham, the programme of events includes world and culturally diverse music concerts. Most notable of the recent events are the Darley Park Saturday World Music Festival and Urban Beats, which featured Classical Friction (a collaboration between Bobby Friction and classical composer Peter Stacey) and Musique et Espectáculo, a fusion of Rai from Abdelkader Saadoun, jazz flute (Keith Waithe) and world music beats. The Three Cities project also brought four international carnival artists to work with community carnival groups, schoolchildren and young people, with a series of special workshops, and various performances at the Caribbean Carnivals of Nottingham, Leicester and Derby.

World In One County Festival
Thoresby Hall
Thoresby Park
Nottinghamshire NG22 9WH
T: 44 (0) 115 974 3734
E: wioc.fest@ntlworld.com
W: www.worldin1county.co.uk
D: Annual, June, two days

A festival of music and dance from round the world, held in Thoresby Park. Previous acts have included Alex Wilson and his Salsa Band, Grand Union and Salmagundi.

London

Atlantic Waves Festival
Calouste Gulbenkian Foundation
98 Portland Place
London W1B 1ET
T: 44 (0) 20 7908 7622
F: 44 (0) 20 7908 7580
E: info@atlanticwaves.org.uk
W: www.atlanticwaves.org.uk
C: Miguel Santos

Annual Portuguese Music festival organised by the Calouste Gulbenkian Foundation covering contemporary jazz, folk, classical and club music. Miguel Santos also presents *Musa Lusa* on Resonance 104.4FM (see Media: Broadcasting).

Coin Street Festival
Bargehouse
Oxo Tower Wharf
Bargehouse Street
South Bank
London SE1 9PH
T: 44 (0) 20 7401 2255
W: www.coinstreetfestival.org

A programme of free summer events which has run for 15 years in the Bernie Spain Gardens near the regenerated Coin Street, next to the South Bank Centre (see Venues and promoters: London). The 2005 programme consisted of several culturally-themed events: *Celebrating Sanctuary*, now in its sixth year, presents musicians, dancers, jugglers, storytellers and holistic practitioners from London's refugee communities and launches the nationwide Refugee Week which celebrates the cultural contribution that refugees and asylum seekers make to UK society. The 2005 festival featured Oi Va Voi and Eastern European gypsy group Szapora. *Carnival de Cuba* celebrates Cuban culture and in 2005 featured UK-based timba player Osvaldo Chacon, Candido Fabre from Havana and ragga and hip hop crew Latin Clan. *Turkish Fest* presented traditional and classical Turkish music including pop star Misa. Coin Street is also part of the Mayor's Thames Festival.

City of London
Bishopsgate Hall
230 Bishopsgate
London EC2M 4HW
T: (0) 20 7377 0540
W: www.colf.org

Primarily a classical music, literature and arts festival, the City of London Festival has also presented a number of international contemporary musicians in some remarkable and unconventional settings around the Square Mile of the City. In 2005 the Soweto Gospel Choir performed in the more classic venue of St Paul's Cathedral whereas Abdul Raheem performed on the concourse of Liverpool Street railway station.

Croydon Summer Festival
Croydon Borough Council
Special Events Office
Croydon Clocktower
Katharine Street
Croydon CR9 1ET
T: 44 (0) 20 8686 4433
E: summerfestival@croydon.gov.uk
W: www.croydon.gov.uk
D: Annual, July, two days

Free two-day outdoor festival organised by Croydon Borough Council and reflecting the culturally diverse community of this area of South London. It has two parts: the World Party and the Croydon Mela. The World Party presents world, jazz and dance acts and included in 2005 Paris-based band Bayefall Gnawa with Senegalese singer Nuru Kane, Ska Cubano from Jamaica and US acid jazz star Roy Ayres. Croydon Mela is in its 10th year and presents a

combination of classical South Asian music, Bhangra and Urban British Asian acts. In 2005 the artists featured included Rizwan-Muazzam Qawwali, Bobby Friction and Nihal, and Birmingham-based Bhangra band DCS.

East London Mela
Club Class Promotions
PO Box 3061
Slough
Berkshire SL3 7ZE
T: 44 (0) 1753 737474
F: 44 (0) 1753 736669
E: info@clubclasspromotions.com
W: www.clubclasspromotions.com
D: Annual, August, one day

East London Mela is a one-day event, taking place (in 2005) at Valentines Park in Ilford. Supported by Barking and Dagenham Borough Council and organised by Club Class Promotions/ United Community Events Ltd, the Mela features a number of well-known Asian stars such as Panjabi Hit Squad and Canadian artist Raghav.

The Greenwich and Docklands International Festival
6 College Approach
London SE10 9HY
T: 44 (0) 20 8305 1818
F: 44 (0) 20 8305 1188
E: admin@festival.org
W: www.festival.org
D: Annual, July, six days

Annual arts festival presenting various events on either side of the Thames in east London. Includes international musicians.

London Jazz Festival
Serious
Chapel House
18 Hatton Place
London EC1N 8RU
T: 44 (0) 20 7405 9900
F: 44 (0) 20 7405 9911
E: info@serious.org.uk
W: www.serious.org.uk
D: Annual, November, c seven days

International jazz festival programmed and organised by Serious (see also Venues and promoters: London, and Agents and managers). Stars in 2005 include Lura from Cape Verde and Seckou Keita.

London Mela
Festivals and Events
Room 3.03
Ealing Town Hall
New Broadway
London W5 2BY
T: 44 (0) 20 8825 6640
E: eiloarts@ealing.gov.uk
W: www.ealing.gov.uk
D: Annual, August, one day

Created in 2003 by the Mayor of London, this free mela is held in West London at Gunnersbury Park as part of Ealing Borough Council's Ealing Summer events programme. It features contemporary and classical music and dance, street theatre, circus, cabaret, comedy, visual arts and the spoken word. In 2005 artists included Susheela Raman and Usha Uthup.

The Mayor's Thames Festival
Bargehouse
Oxo Tower Wharf
Bargehouse Street
South Bank
London SE1 9PH
T: 44 (0) 20 7928 8998
F: 44 (0) 20 7928 2927
E: festivaloffice@coin-street.org
W: www.thamesfestival.org
D: Annual, September, c three days

The annual Thames Festival involves a procession and several arts events. The music programme takes place at several venues, mainly outdoors, and includes weekend events held in conjunction with the Coin Street Festival. Artists appearing in 2005 include Japanese drummers Sonda Eisa, Chilean exiles Bahareque and Latin percussionist Roberto Pla.

Music Village
(See Cultural Co-operation, Venues and promoters: London.)

Notting Hill Carnival
London Notting Hill Carnival (LNHC)
38 Grosvenor Gardens
London SW1W OEB
T: 44 (0) 870 059 1111
W: www.lnhc.org.uk
D: Annual, end of August
(Bank Holiday Weekend)

Notting Hill is a British institution. It is the largest street carnival in Europe, first held in 1964, and celebrating the African and Caribbean cultures of London. It attracts around one million participants and spectators every year. In 2005 the Carnival had the theme 'Unity in diversity' and reflected directly on the London bombing attacks of 7 July. There are five artistic groups at the event: calypsonians, steelbands, masquerade, mobile DJs and static sound systems. It is also a huge tourist attraction: a 2002 study for the London Development Agency estimated that the Notting Hill Carnival generated £93 million annually for London's economy.

Rise Festival

Events for London team
4th floor Greater London Authority
City Hall
The Queen's Walk
London SE1 2AA
T: 44 (0) 20 7983 6554
F: 44 (0) 20 7983 4706
E: info@risefestival.org
W: www.risefestival.org
D: Annual, July, one day

Held in Burgess Park, South East London, and previously known as the Respect Festival, Rise is an anti-racism festival with a multicultural line-up, and is supported by the Mayor of London. It had an attendance of more than 80,000 in 2005. Musical styles covered Turkish, Kurdish, Berber, Middle Eastern pop, desert music and dance by Kurdish and Sufi companies, British Asian acts, drum'n'bass, urban, hip hop and dub. The festival forms part of the Rise Week events in conjunction with other London festivals such as Greenwich and Docklands and several venues.

Spitalfields Festival

75 Brushfield Street
London E1 6AA
T: 44 (0) 20 7377 0287
F: 44 (0) 20 7247 0494
E: info@spitalfieldsfestival.org.uk
W: www.spitalfieldsfestival.org.uk
D: Biannual

The Spitalfields Festival takes place in the regenerated area of London next to the City of London: many of the events are held in the superbly renovated Christ Church, a masterpiece of 18th century architecture. There are two main festivals every year – in the summer and winter. It is mainly a classical music festival featuring small ensembles playing new and early music. Its programme finds room for gospel and jazz and some traditional music from overseas and in particular, of those communities who have made their home in the Spitalfields-Brick Lane area (Jewish music in 2002, French Huguenots in 2003 and Bengali music in 2004).

North East

L'Afrique a Newcastle
Room 112
The Park Centre
Cruddas Park Shopping Centre
Westmoreland Rd
Newcastle upon Tyne NE4 7RW
T: 44 (0) 7956 172099
W: www.lafriqueanewcastle.com
D: Annual, August–September

A festival started in 2003 by L'Afrique en Angleterre, which promotes African music and culture in Tyneside and across the UK. In 2005 they presented Tony Allen, Lokua Kanza (DR Congo) and Petit Pays (Cameroon) and Les Sans Visas at The Sage Gateshead.

Alnwick International Music Festival
119 Allerburn Lea
Alnwick
Northumberland NE66 2QP
T: 44 (0) 1665 510417
W: www.alnwickfestival.com
D: Annual, July–August

Created in 1976, the festival presents many local artists (with a focus on Celtic and Northumbrian artists) alongside folk and traditional artists from a number of countries.

Tyneside Irish Festival
Tyneside Irish Cultural Society
Bridge Hotel
Castle Garth
Newcastle upon Tyne NE1 1RQ
T: 44 (0) 191 2220398
W: tynesideirish.com
D: Annual, October

Irish people represent the largest minority ethnic community in the North East. The Tyneside Irish Festival is a showcase of traditional and contemporary Irish music, dance and culture.

North West

Africa Oyé
Gostin Buildings
32–36 Hanover Street
Liverpool L1 4LN
T: 44 (0) 151 708 6305
E: africa.oye@btconnect.com
W: www.africaoye.com
D: Annual, June, three days

Held in Sefton Park, Liverpool, this major free festival is a showcase of African and Caribbean music. Previous artists appearing include Ba Cissoko (Guinea), Dorbet Gnahore (Ivory Coast), Gangbe Brass Band (Benin), Haja (Madagascar), Kinobe Herbert (Uganda), Hohodza Band (Zimbabwe), Mbilia Bel (DR Congo), General Defao & the Big Stars (DR Congo) and Mthombeni (South Africa). BBC Radio 3 and Merseyside record and broadcast the event.

Eclectica World Music Festival
St Helens Tourist Information Centre
The World of Glass
Chalon Way East
St Helens WA10 1BX
T: 44 (0) 1744 755150
F: 44 (0) 1744 616966
E: info@visitsthelens.com
W: visitsthelens.com
D: Annual, August, one day

Based in Victoria Square, St Helens, this small event features folk, electronica, reggae and world musicians, and in 2005 included Samuel Oyediji from Nigeria and The Kathryn Williams Band. It is part of the St Helens Council's urban regeneration and tourism programme.

Starbucks Manchester Jazz Festival
226 Ducie House
Ducie Street
Manchester M1 2JW
T: 44 (0) 161 228 0662
E: info@manchesterjazz.com
W: www.manchesterjazz.com/home.htm
D: Annual, June, nine days

Large jazz festival, now 10-years-old, featuring a number of international musicians and many Latin jazz groups. The 2005 programme included Descarga (UK/Gibraltar) and Parish (Norway/Sweden). BBC Radio 3's *Jazz on 3* broadcasts the festival live.

South Asian Arts
Chakardar Summer School
Photo: Shamindar Rayatt

Milapfest

Milap Festival Trust
85 Duke Street
Liverpool L1 5AP
T: 44 (0) 151 707 1111 (for all enquiries)
F: 44 (0) 151 707 2425
E: info@milapfest.com
W: www.milapfest.com
T: 44 (0) 151 707 6645 (Samyo)
E: info@samyo.org
W: www.samyo.org
T: 44 (0) 0151 707 6645 (Tarang)
E: info@tarang-uk.org
W: www.tarang-uk.org

Founded in 1985, and now in its 21st year, the
Milap Festival Trust is a South Asian Arts Festival
and Development Agency covering music and
dance. The organisation creates artistic
collaborations, commissions and tours in Liverpool,
Manchester, London and nationally. It has a close
relationship with the Philharmonic Hall,
Liverpool (see Venues and promoters: North
West). Recent events include Ravi and Anoushka
Shankar and sarod master Ustad Amjad Ali Khan.
The Milap Festival Trust also runs an extensive
education programme: in 2002, in collaboration
with the South Asian Music Consortium, it
formed Samyo (the South Asian Youth Orchestra)
a 20-strong ensemble of musicians between 10
to 18-years-old. It also manages Tarang (the
National South Asian Music Ensemble) for
musicians over 18. Both are designed to provide
British South Asian musicians with performance
opportunities in the early development of their
careers and are supported by Arts Council England.

x.trax

51 Old Birley Street
Hulme
Manchester M15 5RF
T: 44 (0) 161 227 8383
F: 44 (0) 161 342 0741
E: info@xtrax.org.uk
W: www.xtrax.org.uk
C: Maggie Clarke, Director
D: Biennially, June, three days

x.trax is the largest international showcase
festival in the UK and covers drama, dance and
music to an invited audience of arts promoters,
festival and arts professionals, as well as local
audiences. From May 2003 x.trax have worked
with Arts Council England's decibel project to
present a showcase of British-based culturally
diverse performance. The programme featured
80 artists and companies of African, Asian and
Caribbean descent, presenting theatre, dance,
music, live art and street shows. In 2005, musicians
involved included British-born Chinese violinists
Chi2, Dennis Rollins, UK kora player Seckou Keita
and multi-instrumentalist Tunde Jegede.

South East

Brighton Festival
12a Pavilion Buildings
Castle Square
Brighton BN1 1EE
T: 44 (0) 1273 709709 (ticket office)
W: www.brighton-festival.org.uk
D: Annual, May, two days

The Brighton Festival is the largest international multi-artform festival in England and will celebrate its 40th anniversary in 2006. Many of the music events take place at the Brighton Dome (see Venues and promoters: South East). The festival presents classical, jazz, world and folk music, and commissions some work itself.

Broadstairs Folk Week
Pierremont Hall
Broadstairs
Kent CT10 1JX
T: 44 (0) 1843 604080
F: 44 (0) 1843 866422
E: info@broadstairsfolkweek.org.uk
W: www.broadstairsfolkweek.org.uk
D: Annual, August

Large folk festival featuring many international acts from Canada, the States, Australia, New Zealand and Europe, and including an extensive workshop programme for adults and children.

A Big Day Out/Out There
South Hill Park Arts Centre
Ringmead
Birch Hill
Bracknell RG12 7PA
T: 44 (0) 1344 484858
F: 44 (0) 1344 411427
E: enquiries@southhillpark.org.uk
W: www.outtherefestival.co.uk
W: www.southhillpark.org.uk

Based at South Hill Park in Bracknell (an 18th century mansion), A Big Day Out will replace the Out There festival in 2006 as part of the Bracknell Festival. Out There has presented many world music acts in the past and is often described as a 'mini WOMAD'.

Pestalozzi International Village
Sedlescombe
Battle
East Sussex TN33 0RR
T: 44 (0) 1424 870444
F: 44 (0) 1424 870655
E: office@pestalozzi.org.uk
W: www.pestalozzi.org.uk

Created by Swiss humanist Dr Walter Corti in the aftermath of World War II and inspired by the work of early 19th Century humanist Johann Heinrich Pestalozzi, the Pestalozzi Villages are an international movement dedicated to providing opportunities to students aged 16 upwards from low-income families in Asia and Africa. The Village and its support groups host a number of festivals and events throughout the year. The largest, the Global Fusion event in 2005, included Dhol Foundation, Ghanaian percussionist Nana Tsiboe and mbira player Anna Mudeka.

Towersey Village Festival
Festival office
PO Box 296
Matlock
Derbyshire DE4 3XU
E: info@towerseyfestival.com
W: www.towerseyfestival.com/tarena.html
D: Annual, August, five days

Towersey, a small town in Oxfordshire, has held this major folk arts festival for 41 years. The festival programmes folk and roots music, dance, workshops and a Children's Festival.

WOMAD (World of Music, Arts and Dance)
Mill Lane, Box
Corsham
Wiltshire SN13 8PN
T: 44 (0) 1225 744494
F: 44 (0) 1225 743481
E: info@womad.org
W: http://womad.org
C: Thomas Brooman, Artistic Director
C: Paula Henderson, Events Manager

Created in 1980 by Peter Gabriel, the first WOMAD festival was held in Shepton Mallett in 1982. It has grown into the most important world music festival in the UK. From the late 1980s, WOMAD started touring nationally and internationally (to over 20 countries) and now holds regular annual events in a number of holiday destinations around the world including Australia (WOMADelaide), New Zealand,

Singapore, the Canary Islands, Sicily and the UK each year. Its main event, WOMAD Rivermead, is held in July in Reading and usually lasts three days. The 2005 event presented Youssou N'Dour et le Super Etoile de Dakar, Mahmoud Ahmed from Ethiopia, superstars Amadou and Mariam from Mali, Apache Indian and The Reggae Revolution from the UK, and Nusrat Fateh Ali Khan's nephews, the Rizwan-Muazzam Qawwali of Pakistan. The line-up also included Robert Plant and The Strange Sensation. BBC Radio 3 broadcasts live from the event. The website has an online shop selling records, DVDs, clothing, tickets to all WOMAD events and other merchandise.

In 1983 the WOMAD Foundation was set up as the charitable arm of the festival. The Foundation engages in educational work and cultural exchange involving music and range of other artforms (including the visual arts), and focuses on bringing young people and professional musicians and singers into contact with each other, especially artists who have left their country of origin. A considerable amount of the Foundation's work is curriculum oriented. See also Real World Records (Labels and distributors).

South West

Ashton Court Festival

1 Ninetree Hill
Stokes Croft
Bristol BS1 3SB
T: 44 (0) 117 904 2275
F: 44 (0) 117 904 2276
E: info@ashtoncourtfestival.com
W: www.ashtoncourtfestival.co.uk
D: Annual, July

Bristol-based festival involving national and local talent and a Global Marquee (programmed with Colston Hall (see Venues and promoters: South West) which showcases a mix of world music and international acts.

Bath Fringe Festival

103 Walcot Street
Bath BA1 5BW
E: admin@bathfringe.co.uk
W: www.bathfringe.co.uk
D: Annual, May–June

Views differ on when the Fringe started, but the semi-official date is 1991. It now presents a large, multi-artform programme of 150 events over 17 days, most of which are self-promoting that run in parallel to the Bath International Music Festival. The Fringe books only about 20% of the acts itself. The 2005 Fringe included Turkish bellydancing, Latin, and a performance by Moussa Kouyate and Kevin Brown.

Bath International Music Festival

5 Broad Street
Bath BA1 5LJ
T: 44 (0) 1225 462231
F: 44 (0) 1225 445551
E: info@bathfestivals.org.uk
W: www.bathmusicfest.org.uk
C: Joanna MacGregor, Artistic Director
C: Nod Knowles, Chief Executive
D: Annual, May–June, two weeks

Established in 1955, this music festival is predominantly classical, but it also programmes jazz and world music in its Contemporary and World Music Weekends. In 2005 the festival presented artists such as Susheela Raman and tabla player Yogesh Samsi. See also Bath Fringe Festival.

Glastonbury Festival of contemporary performing arts

Glastonbury Festival Office
28 Northload Street
Glastonbury
Somerset BA6 9JJ
T: 44 (0) 1458 834 596
F: 44 (0) 1458 833 235
E: office@glastonburyfestivals.co.uk
W: www.glastonburyfestivals.co.uk
D: Note – there will be no festival in 2006

The largest greenfield music festival in the world with 150,000 attendees. World music has always been a feature of the event: WOMAD first ran a stage there in 1987. The JazzWorld Stage has a big reputation, and in 2005 presented Baaba Maal and Femi Kuti.

Golowan Festival
Golowan Community Arts Trust
The Barbican
Battery Road
Penzance
Cornwall TR18 4EF
T: 44 (0) 1736 332211
E: info@golowan.com
W: www.golowan.com

With its roots in pagan rituals to celebrate Midsummer Day, the Summer Solstice and the Feast of St John the Baptist, the Golowan Festival in Penzance focuses on traditional Cornish arts and music and a substantial world music offering (including artists from Latin America and Rajasthan in 2005).

Larmer Tree
PO Box 1790
Salisbury
Wiltshire SP5 5WA
T: 44 (0) 1725 552300
F: 44 (0) 1725 553090
W: www.larmertreefestival.com
D: Annual, July

A festival held in the beautiful Pitt-Rivers Estate of Larmer Tree at Tollard Royal Wiltshire, and presenting an eclectic programme of folk, jazz, funk, rock, blues and world music which included, in 2005, Balkan music, Javanese gamelan and many UK-based musicians playing fusion, Bhangra and Americana.

Shambala
17 The Coach House
2 Upper York Street
Bristol BS2 8QN
E: music@shambalafestival.org (music enquiries)
E: office@shambalafestival.org (general enquiries)
W: www.shambalafestival.org
D: Annual, August

Festival in Devon, presenting funk, folk, African, Latin, Asian, blues, hip hop, reggae, samba, singer-songwriters, jazz, beats, classical, and as they put it, 'weird stuff'.

Sidmouth Folk Week
Tourist Information Centre
Sidmouth
Devon EX10 8XR
T: 44 (0) 1395 516441
E: info@sidmouthfolkweek.co.uk
W: www.sidmouthfolkweek.co.uk
D: Annual, July–August, eight days

After 50 years, the Sidmouth Folk Festival closed in 2004 because of problems with (of all things) wet weather insurance. A group of Devon promoters including Folk South West, some local businesses and the local council came together and took on the festival as a consortium. The 2005 programme had 300 events involving the usual mix of folk, roots and world, including 'festival favourites' Black Umfolosi from Zimbabwe.

The Swindon Mela
c/o Premier House
Station Road
Swindon SN1 1TZ
T: 44 (0) 1793 530328
E: trathbone@swindon.gov.uk
W: www.swindonmela.comv
D: Annual, July, one day

Free annual mela run by Swindon Borough
Council attracting some 20,000 people and
programming a mix of UK Asian talent in fusion
and classical styles.

Trowbridge Village Pump Festival
PO Box 984
Bath
Avon BA1 6YH
T: 44 (0) 1225 769132
E: enquiries@trowbridgefestival.co.uk
W: www.trowbridgefestival.co.uk
D: Annual, July, four days

Village festival featuring folk and roots music. The
2005 programme included Galician Xosé Manuel
Budiño and Dutch blues guitarist Hans Theessink.

WOMAD (World of Music, Arts and Dance)
(The WOMAD festival takes place in Reading, see
Festivals: South East.)

Wychwood Music Festival
Wychwood Festivals
PO Box 1000
Cheltenham GL53 9WY
T: 44 (0) 1242 244944
E: info@wychwoodfestival.com
W: www.wychwoodfestival.com
D: Annual, June

A new (2005) world and roots music festival near
Cheltenham. Its large programme of international
and UK artists included Candido Fabre Y Su Banda
from Cuba, Mory Kante, Gilles Peterson, Mercan
Dede, Mabulu from Mozambique, Rita Ray and
Max Reinhardt (The Shrine).

West Midlands

The Big Chill
Chillfest Ltd
PO Box 52707
London EC2P 2WE
T: 44 (0) 20 7684 2020
E: info@bigchill.net
W: www.bigchill.net
D: Annual, August, three days

The Big Chill Festival takes place at Eastnor Castle near Ledbury, Herefordshire. The festival, which attracts 30,000 attendees is programmed by DJ Pete Lawrence and includes many international club, world and global dance artists. Previous stars have included Röyksopp, Ralph Myerz and the Jack Herren Band, DJ Patife (Brazil), Kruder and Dorfmiester, Oi Va Voi, Gilles Peterson and Jazzanova.

Birmingham Eid Mela
Birmingham City Council
The Council House
Victoria Square
Birmingham B1 1BB
T: 44 (0) 121 303 9944
E: contact@birmingham.gov.uk
W: www.birmingham.gov.uk
D: Annual, June, one day

Held in Cannon Hill Park, the Mela attracts around 30,000 visitors and is organised by Birmingham's Muslim communities and Birmingham City Council as a showcase for Islamic arts and culture. Local and international acts are presented such as Abdelkader Saadoun, Navi and the Kashmiri Folk Band.

Rupinder Phull performing at SABHA, **sampad**'s monthly Birmingham showcase
Photo: Buzby Bywater

Lichfield Festival
7 The Close
Lichfield
Staffordshire WS13 7LD
T: 44 (0) 1543 306270
E: festivaloffice@lichfield-arts.org.uk
W: www.lichfieldfestival.org
D: Annual, July, 10 days

The Lichfield Festival has a predominantly classical programme, which includes world and folk music such as Tibetan monks, the Bollywood Brass Band, The Tord Gustavsen Trio and the Conservatoire Folk Ensemble who draw on English, Celtic and European folk traditions.

Starbucks Birmingham International Jazz Festival
PO Box 944
Birmingham B16 8UT
T: 44 (0) 121 454 7020
W: www.bigbearmusic.com/festival/festival.html

Large jazz event with international guests such as (in 2005) Olga Skrancova (Czech Republic), Oriental Jazz Band (Holland) and Hiromi (Japan).

Off the Tracks Festival
PO Box 68
Derby DE1 3XY
T: 44 (0) 1332 384518
W: www.offthetracks.co.uk
D: Annual, September, three days

Off the Tracks offers folk, roots, dance and fusion on two stages. Artists in 2005 included the Taal Tabla Ensemble, Oojami and DJ AJ.

Yorkshire

Beverley and East Riding Folk Festival
Festival Office
PO Box 296
Matlock
Derbyshire DE4 3XU
T: 44 (0) 1629 827019
F: 44 (0) 1629 821874
E: info@beverleyfestival.com
W: www.beverleyfestival.com
C: Chris Wade, Director
D: Annual, June, three days

Folk festival programmed by Chris Wade of Adastra (see Agents and managers) in Beverley, five miles north of Hull, offering a number of world music artists. Previous artists include the Warsaw Village Band and Black Umfolosi.

Bradford Mela
Wool Exchange
Hustlergate
Bradford
West Yorkshire BD1 1RE
E: info@bradfordfestival.yorks.com
W: www.bradfordfestival.com/mela.htm
T: 44 (0) 1274 309199
F: 44 (0) 1274 724213
D: Annual, July

First held in 1987, the Bradford Mela is the largest in Britain with over 300,000 attendees in Peel Park. It is held to coincide with the Bradford Festival. The programme mixes local and international acts playing traditional, fusion and dance music such as Faakhir from Pakistan, sufi group Rizwan-Muazzam Qawwali, and the Talvin Singh Trio.

FuseLeeds
Leeds International Concert Season
PO Box 596
Leeds Town Hall
Leeds LS2 8YQ
T: 44 (0) 113 395 1244
E: info@fuseleeds.org.uk
W: www.fuseleeds.org.uk

Biennial contemporary music festival, which also runs year-round showcase and concert events of jazz, contemporary, rock, folk and classical music.

Harrogate International Festival
1 Victoria Avenue
Harrogate HG1 1EQ
T: 44 (0) 1423 562303
F: 44 (0) 1423 521264
E: info@harrogate-festival.org.uk
W: www.harrogate-festival.org.uk
D: Annual, July–August

Founded in 1966, the festival, now in its 40th year has an extensive jazz and world strand to its programme. In 2005, artists included Youssou N'Dour et le Super Etoile de Dakar, and the Afro Cuban All Stars.

Huddersfield Contemporary Music Festival
Music Department
University of Huddersfield
Huddersfield HD1 3DH
T: 44 (0) 1484 425082
F: 44 (0) 1484 472957
E: info@hcmf.co.uk
W: www.hcmf.co.uk
C: Alison Povey, Festival Manager
D: Annual, November

Primarily a festival of contemporary classical music, Huddersfield also presents world, electronica, dance and traditional music from places as diverse as Taiwan and Tunisia.

Hull Jazz Festival
Hull City Council
Guildhall
Hull HU1 2AA
T: 44 (0) 1482 300300
E: info@hullcc.gov.uk
W: www.hullcc.gov.uk/jazz
D: Annual, July–August, 7 days

Now in its 13th year, the Hull Jazz Festival presents a number of international acts every year. 2005 included Gilad Atzmon and the Louis Stewart Quartet.

WOMAD Rivermead Festival 2005, Reading
Photo: Jonathan Hill

Swaledale Festival

Hudson House
Reeth, nr Richmond
North Yorkshire DL11 6TB
T: 44 (0) 1748 880018
F: 44 (0) 1748 880028
E: info@swaledale-festival.org.uk
W: www.swaledale-festival.org.uk
D: Annual, May–June

A festival in the heart of the Yorkshire Dales, Swaledale is now in its 25th year. It presents a mix of folk and international musics including (in 2005) Venezuelan pianist Elena Riu's Salsa Nueva, Eastern European gypsy band ZUM and the London-based Grand Union Band presenting Caribbean, South American and African jazz. The festival has a substantial educational programme and works closely with the North Yorkshire Youth Music Action Zone.

Whitby Musicport

The Port Hole
16 Skinner Street
Whitby YO21 3AJ
T: 44 (0) 1947 603475
F: 44 (0) 1947 603509
E: artistes@whitbymusicport.com
W: www.musicport.fsnet.co.uk
D: Annual, October

World music festival held at the Whitby Pavilion. In addition to the festival, Whitby Musicport presents a series of concerts throughout the year at The Compass Club, Whitby. Artists in 2005 include Yat-Kha, Talvin Singh (Tabtek) and Los de Abajo.

Media

Books and reference guides

Direct Roots
c/o Mrs Casey Music
PO Box 296
Matlock
Derbyshire DE4 3XU
E: info@folkarts-england.org
W: www.folkarts-england.org

The most comprehensive guide to folk, roots and related music and arts in the British Isles. Its third edition is expected in 2006.

Rough Guides
62–70 Shorts Gardens
London WC2H 9AH
W: www.roughguides.com

Rough Guides publish travel books to over 150 destinations and many other thematically-focused books. *The Rough Guide to World Music* was first published in two volumes in 1999. It is the most comprehensive publication on the subject.

Ivo Papasov, winner of
BBC Radio 3 World Music
Audience Award, 2005
Photo: Mark Pinder

Broadcasting

British Broadcasting Corporation
Broadcasting House
London W1A 1AA
W: www.bbc.co.uk/radio

The BBC is a public service broadcasting company, which is financed by licence fees levied on all households and businesses that own television receivers, bringing in around £3 billion per annum. It carries no advertising. BBC TV consists of two national channels (1 and 2) plus two extra (3 and 4) on digital television, BBC News and BBC Worldwide, plus local television channels and the BBC Parliament channel. There are five national radio networks (Radios 1, 2, 3, 4 and Five Live), five digital national networks (Asian Network, 6music, BBC7, Five Live Sports Extra, 1Xtra), three national services (Radio Scotland, Ulster and Wales) and 43 local radio stations in England. BBC Radio represents over 50% of all UK radio broadcasting. A selection of its channels follows.

BBC 1Xtra
W: www.bbc.co.uk/1xtra

BBC digital radio station, also available on the internet, specialising in urban and Black music (including Asian sounds) from around the world and targeted at a young (under-25) audience, particularly – but not exclusively – young African Caribbean listeners. Its playlists include live performances recorded all over the world.

BBC Asian Network

W: www.bbc.co.uk/asiannetwork

The BBC Asian Network is a speech and music network broadcast in several Asian languages and English on digital radio, the internet and AM radio with an audience of about 500,000. Its music output includes DJ Adil Ray's show five nights a week (including live performances from time to time); Navinder Bhogal's afternoon shows; Sanjay Sharma's cultural programme, *Hindi/Urdu*, and the British Asian Album Chart presented by Bobby Friction. The network has several agreements with major Asian labels enabling it to play new tracks up to two weeks before general release. It also promotes club nights and concerts (such as the March 2005 event at the Symphony Hall, Birmingham).

BBC Four (tv)

W: www.bbc.co.uk/bbcfour

Digital BBC TV channel offering arts-oriented programming. World music is well represented with concerts, profiles and interviews with musicians, and special programmes such as the *Africa Live* concert from Dakar (in aid of the Roll Back Malaria campaign), *The African Rock 'n' Roll Years* – a documentary history of African music and highlights of the Festival in the Desert 2004.

BBC London

W: www.bbc.co.uk/london

Local London radio station (on 94.9FM, the internet, and digital radio. Charlie Gillett's radio show broadcasts every Saturday night and features such things as games of live and unrehearsed Radio Ping-Pong (Gillett and a guest play records back to back, reflecting and contrasting artists and songs).

BBC Radio 1

W: www.bbc.co.uk/radio1

BBC Radio 1 has been a mainstay of British popular music for 40 years (broadcasting on 97–99 FM, digital and internet). Bobby Friction and Nihal's British Asian music show goes out every Wednesday night, 9pm–11pm and Gilles Peterson (the man who invented Acid Jazz) presents *Worldwide*, a global music show on Sundays.

BBC Radio 3

W: www.bbc.co.uk/radio3

On 90–93FM, digital radio and the internet, the BBC's classical music channel is the UK's most consistent broadcaster of world music. Aside from its sponsorship of the Awards for World Music, it has a portfolio of knowledgeable presenters. *World Routes* is a mix of interviews with musicians, live concerts, a monthly record round-up, and special location features. Its presenter Lucy Duran is a former curator of the National Sound Archive and since 1992 lecturer at London University's School of Oriental and African Studies (SOAS). Fiona Talkington and Verity Sharp co-present *Late Junction* every week night covering an eclectic mix of contemporary and traditional music from around the world. Andy Kershaw's show began on Radio 3 in April 2001 following his sacking from Radio 1. His Radio 3 show (on Sundays, weekly) is equally influential. The Radio 3 website also has an archive of BBC recordings of world music concerts.

BBC World On Your Street

W: www.bbc.co.uk/radio3/world/onyourstreet

This website celebrates world music in the UK, from touring international artists to the wealth of diasporic and ethnically diverse musicians based here in the UK. It incorporates the BBC Africa On Your Street project.

BBC World Service

W: www.bbc.co.uk/worldservice

The BBC's World Service is not financed by licence fees but by the Foreign & Commonwealth Office (see Government departments). It was created in 1988 by a merger of various overseas broadcasting units within the BBC. It broadcasts in over 40 languages. And carries a number of world music oriented programmes, including ones presented by Charlie Gillett.

Bellowhead – Off-Womex Showcase artists
Photo: Matt Thomas

Independent radio stations

Choice FM
W: www.choicefm.com

Urban music radio channel (also on digital as Urban Choice). The Saturday/Sunday 12am –3am *International Link-Up* programme (between the UK, the Bahamas, Jamaica and the USA) brings together Soul, Reggae, Soca, Dancehall, R&B and Hip Hop from the four locations.

Jazz FM
W: www.jazzfm.com

UK radio station specialising in jazz and including many world jazz artists. (Digital, internet and FM).

Kiss
W: www.kiss100.com

Urban music station. DJ and producer Rishi Rich presents British Urban-Desi beats on Sunday nights.

Resonance FM
W: www.resonancefm.com

Resonance 104.4FM is London's first radio art station, run by London Musicians' Collective (see Support bodies). Shows include *Musa Lusa* presented by Miguel Santos, a programme of music from Portugal (club, fado, experimental electronica, alternative pop etc). Also available on the internet.

Spectrum Radio
W: www.spectrumradio.net

A London-based station (also available on digital and the internet) that specialises in broadcasting to what are considered niche communities. It offers a wide range of music from around the world.

Xfm
W: www.xfm.co.uk

DJ Nick Luscombe's *Flo-Motion* show every Sunday night features many global club stars.

Journals and magazines

fRoots
PO Box 337
London N4 1TW
T: 44 (0) 20 8340 9651
F: 44 (0) 20 8348 5626
E: froots@frootsmag.com
W: www.frootsmag.com
C: Ian Anderson, Editor

fRoots, which is published monthly, has been around for 25 years and covers the folk, roots and world sector. It has a readership of around 40,000 (circulation of 11,000). The magazine is an invaluable source of information on what is happening in the UK sector and the *fRoots* website contains a detailed archive of previous features and reviews.

MOJO
Mappin House
4 Winsley Street
London W1W 8HF
T: 44 (0) 20 7436 1515
F: 44 (0) 20 7312 8296
E: mojo@emap.com
W: www.mojo4music.com

Monthly rock magazine covering a wide range of music. It also runs a digital radio station.

NME (New Musical Express)
King's Reach Tower
Stamford Street
London SE1 9LS
T: 44 (0) 870 444 5000
W: www.nme.co.uk/magazine

UK weekly magazine which has influenced many generations with its coverage of new releases, tours and special features on popular music.

Songlines
PO Box 54209
London W14 0WU
T: 44 (0) 20 7371 2777
F: 44 (0) 20 7371 2220
E: info@songlines.co.uk
W: www.songlines.co.uk
C: Simon Broughton, Editor

Songlines is published six times a year and covers traditional, contemporary and fusion world music. It is edited by Simon Broughton, co-editor of *The Rough Guide to World Music*, and columnists include Andy Kershaw. *Songlines* runs a very useful listing of retail outlets all over Britain that contribute to *Songlines* World Music Chart.

Straight No Chaser
17d Ellingfort Road
London E8 3PA
T: 44 (0) 20 8533 9999
F: 44 (0) 20 8985 6447
E: info@straightnochaser.co.uk
W: www.straightnochaser.co.uk

UK music magazine focusing on 'inter-planetary sounds'.

The Wire
23 Jack's Place
6 Corbet Place
London E1 6NN
T: 44 (0) 20 7422 5014
F: 44 (0) 20 7422 5011
W: www.thewire.co.uk

A monthly music magazine covering progressive, adventurous and non-mainstream musics.

Websites

Africa Centre

www.africadatabase.org

Maintained by the Africa Centre (see Support bodies), the Contemporary Africa Database contains information on individuals and organisations all over the world and is funded by the Rockefeller Foundation.

Arts Council England

www.artscouncil.org.uk/links

An extensive listing of all Arts Council regularly funded organisations and other bodies in all genres.

BBC World Music

www.bbc.co.uk/music/world

A good 'hub' website bringing together the BBC's various world music sites online, along with news and reviews.

Charlie Gillett

www.charliegillett.com

Website maintained by the eponymous BBC Radio London DJ Charlie Gillett with news, views and reviews related to world music.

Creativexport

www.creativexport.co.uk

This website, which is regularly updated, is supported by the British Council Arts, Science and Creative Industries Department, UK Trade & Investment and the DCMS and provides information on funding, market research and contacts for all sectors of the creative industries, plus an extensive listing of music showcases, festivals, training opportunities and other useful music-sector information.

culturebase.net

www.culturebase.net

A database of international artists which includes many non-European musicians and composers who have been presented in Europe. The database can be searched by genre, instrument, country or by name of the artist. A large listing of links to similar websites is also included.

Department for Culture, Media and Sport

www.culture.gov.uk

UK government department with responsibility for the National Lottery, and arts and heritage in England. Website includes information on funding in the UK.

Fly global music culture

www.fly.co.uk

A website for global music culture activists containing news and reviews.

i-UK

www.i-uk.com

A useful general guide to the UK, including information on visa and work permits, regional information and an arts and cultural overview with links to many organisations and websites working in music.

Jazz Services

www.jazzservices.org.uk

Listing of jazz organisations with many world music organisations also included.

London: Diaspora Capital

www.culturalco-operation.org

A searchable database of artists from the various culturally diverse communities resident in London compiled by Cultural Co-operation.

Visiting Arts

www.visitingarts.org.uk/festivals1.html

(See the main entry in Support bodies.) Along with many other useful online resources (including tips to overseas music practitioners and managers wishing to work in the UK) Visiting Arts lists UK-based arts festivals that regularly programme international work (including all genres of music).

Tinariwen – African Soul Rebels UK Tour
Photo: Eric Mulet

Support bodies (national and regional)

Africa Centre
38 King Street
Covent Garden
London WC2E
T: 44 (0) 20 7836 1973
F: 44 (0) 20 7836 1975
E: info@africacentre.org.uk
W: www.africacentre.org.uk

Founded in 1961, the Africa Centre aims to create a greater awareness among British and other European people about developments in Africa and its diaspora. The Centre houses a hall, library and art gallery. It programmes visual arts, literature, film and music (and other genres) and promotes an education programme. A radio show *Talking Africa* is produced for Spectrum Radio. And the Centre's website provides access to the Contemporary Africa Database of individuals and organisations.

African & Caribbean Music Circuit (ACMC)
Suite N3–7
Charles House
375 Kensington High Street
London W14 8QH
T: 44 (0) 20 7602 7379
F: 44 (0) 20 7602 9182
E: info@acmc.uk.com
W: www.acmc.uk.com
C: Charles Easmon

ACMC arranges tours from Africa and the Caribbean, of African, contemporary, fusion, Latin, rap, soul, vocal, world and funk music and is funded by Arts Council England to act as a national agency. It works in collaboration with a number of organisations, most recently with the School of Oriental and African Studies Summer School. It represents a number of bands such as Misty in Roots and the River Niger Orchestra. Its educational work is community-based and combines academic and practical elements (hands-on tuition via workshops, residencies and master-classes) as well as specially-designed work packs and worksheets.

Susheela Raman
Photo: Robert Leslie

Asian Music Circuit (AMC)
Ground Floor
Unit E
West Point
33/34 Warple Way
London W3 0RG
T: 44 (0) 20 8742 9911
F: 44 (0) 20 8749 3948
E: info@amc.org.uk
W: www.amc.org.uk

Set up in 1989 by the Arts Council of Great Britain, the AMC is one of the leading promoters of Asian music and music of the Far East in the UK. It also offers an advisory service to musicians, institutions and promoters working with Asian artists. Its core business is as a tour manager and it manages a number of educational activities including seminars, lectures, recordings, videos and exhibitions. The AMC focuses on the whole of Asia with particular emphasis on South Asia, and presents classical and contemporary musicians from a wide range of genres. A substantial capital project is under way to create an Asian Music Centre, which will contain its large collection of musical instruments, digital audiovisual archives and interactive multimedia facilities.

Association of British Calypsonians
Yaa Asantewaa Arts and Community Centre
1 Chippenham Mews
Chippenham Road
London W9 2AN
T: 44 (0) 20 7286 1656
F: 44 (0) 20 7266 0377
E: yaa@yaaasant.demon.co.uk
W: www.yaaasant.demon.co.uk

Formed in 1991 the Association of British Calypsonians (ABC) is the representative body for calypso and soca music in the UK and Europe. ABC produces educational programmes and cultural events concerning the history and tradition of calypso. It works closely with the Notting Hill Carnival in association with the Yaa Asantewaa Carnival Group and the African & Caribbean Music Circuit.

Association of Independent Music (AIM)
Lamb House
Church Street
London W4 2PD
T: 44 (0) 20 8994 5599
F: 44 (0) 20 8994 5222
E: info@musicindie.com
W: www.musicindie.org

AIM is a non-profit trade body established in 1998 by UK independent record labels to represent the independent record sector, which represents about a quarter of the value of the total UK market (£2 billion in 2003). There are about 900 members, all of whom are UK-based independent record labels or distributors. AIM organises trade delegations to events such as Popkomm and Midem, and is active in international networking. And it provides targeted advice on business start up, marketing, legal issues, matters connected with music downloads (AIM Digital) and acts as a government lobby organisation.

Association of Festival Organisers
PO Box 296
Matlock
Derbyshire DE4 3XU
T: 44 (0) 1629 827014
F: 44 (0) 1629 821874
E: info@folkarts-england.org
W: www.afouk.org

Umbrella body formed in 1987 which provides a channel of communication between festivals and events of all kinds including early music, bluegrass, cajun, step and clog, dance, world music and folk arts. It presents an annual conference. (See also FolkArts England in this section.)

Bharatiya Vidya Bhavan (Bhavan Centre)
4a Castletown Road
West Kensington
London W14 9HE
T: 44 (0) 20 7381 3086
F: 44 (0) 20 7381 8758
E: info@bhavan.net
W: www.bhavan.net

Also known as the Bhavan Centre, this is the largest institute for Indian art and culture outside India and provides courses of music, dance, languages, yoga and drama to around 800 students. Its Mountbatten Hall is a 200-seat auditorium which is undergoing a renovation.

British Association of Steelbands (BAS)
Tabernacle
Powys Square
London W11 2AY
T: 44 (0) 20 7351 6719
W: www.panpodium.com
C: Debi Gardner

Provides a range of resources including funding for performances, training, new arrangements, and the perennial problem of tuning.

BPI (British Phonographic Industry)
Riverside Building
County Hall
Westminster Bridge Road
London SE1 7JA
T: 44 (0) 20 7803 1300
F: 44 (0) 20 7803 1310
E: general@bpi.co.uk
E: antipiracy@bpi.co.uk
W: www.bpi.co.uk

The BPI is the British record industry's trade association and was founded in 1973 to fight the growing problem of music piracy. Its membership of 320 includes record companies, manufacturers and distributors. It publishes data and statistics on UK records sales by sector, runs training programmes, promotes networking events, provides legal support and organises the industry's annual showcase event the BRIT Awards (See Competitions and awards). Working with UK Trade & Investment (see Statutory agencies) it also helps to promote international sales of British music.

Chinese Arts Centre
Market Buildings
Thomas Street
Manchester M4 1EU
T: 44 (0) 161 832 7271
F: 44 (0) 161 832 7513
E: info@chinese-arts-centre.org
W: www.chinese-arts-centre.org

Manchester has a substantial Chinese community. The centre opened in 1986 as the UK agency for the promotion of contemporary Chinese art and interpretation of Chinese culture.

Community Music Ltd
82 Southwark Bridge Road
London SE1 0AS
T: 44 (0) 20 7633 0550
F: 44 (0) 20 7261 1133
E: everyone@cmonline.org.uk
W: www.cmonline.org.uk

CM is a music charity which offers education, training and artist support programmes for musicians, especially young people who have not enjoyed mainstream educational opportunities. CM offers an annual programme of activities ranging from weekend classes for 7 to 16-year-olds through to full-time undergraduate production and teaching courses. They support recording, production and promotional opportunities for young artists, offer advice from the music industry, and assist with new business start ups particularly those in the not-for-profit sector. Its educational programmes involve artists such as Courtney Pine, Asian Dub Foundation, PyrotechnicRadio.com, BreakFasterz, and many others.

Contemporary Music Network (CMN)
Music Department
Arts Council England
14 Great Peter Street
London SW1P 3NQ
T: 44 (0) 20 7973 6504
F: 44 (0) 20 7973 6983
W: www.cmntours.org.uk

An agency within Arts Council England, created in 1971, which acts as an in-house promoter organising around 12 tours per year in England (and into Scotland, Wales and Northern Ireland) of jazz, world music, experimental, electronica, folk, pop and music beyond the mainstream. Projects are selected via an application process (deadline is usually May in the year prior to the proposed tour). Projects are usually collaborative in nature and should be new commissions or premiers. Tours are generally about a week in duration. Applications are open to British and international artists (international artists must have a UK-based promoter). An application form is available from their website.

Creative Partnerships
14 Great Peter Street
London SW1P 3NQ
T: 44 (0) 845 300 6200 (enquiries)
F: 44 (0) 20 7973 6590
Textphone: 44 (0) 20 7973 6564
E: enquiries@artscouncil.org.uk
W: www.creativepartnerships.com

Creative Partnerships is a joint initiative funded by the Department for Culture, Media and Sport and the Department for Education and Skills, and is run by Arts Council England (see Statutory agencies). It provides schoolchildren across England with the opportunity to develop creativity in learning and to take part in cultural activities of the highest quality. There are 16 local partnerships around the country, with a further 20 being introduced in the next two years. The partnerships arrange and assist UK and foreign artists to work in schools and for local teachers to travel. Its music work is carried out in partnership with Youth Music (see the end of this section).

English Folk Dance and Song Society (EFDSS)
Cecil Sharp House
2 Regents Park Road
London NW1 7AY
T: 44 (0) 20 7485 2206
F: 44 (0) 20 7284 0534
E: info@efdss.org
W: www.efdss.org

Founded in 1932, the EFDSS encouraged or created many UK folk festivals. It maintains the Vaughan Williams Memorial Library as the country's national archive and resource centre for folk music, dance and song.

FolkArts England
PO Box 296
Matlock
Derbyshire DE4 3XU
T: 44 (0) 1629 827014
F: 44 (0) 1629 821874
E: info@folkarts-england.org
W: www.folkarts-england.org

FolkArts England is a national development agency for folk, roots, traditional and acoustic music in England and incorporates the Association of Festival Organisers, FolkArts Network, Shooting Roots (youth project) and *Direct Roots* directory, the guide to folk, roots and related music and arts in the British Isles.

Folkworks
(See entry for The Sage Gateshead in Venues and promoters: North East.)

Jazz Services
First Floor
132 Southwark Street
London SE1 0SW
T: 44 (0) 20 7928 9089
F: 44 (0) 20 7401 6870
E: admin@jazzservices.org.uk
W: www.jazzservices.org.uk

A networking and support organisation for jazz in the UK. Working with organisations such as the PRS Foundation (see later in this section) and Arts Council England, it provides information, advice, guidance and a range of services including the most comprehensive database on the UK jazz scene which is accessible via their website.

Kuumba
Arts & Community Resource Centre
20–23 Hepburn Road
St Paul's
Bristol BS2 8UD
T: 44 (0) 117 942 1870
F: 44 (0) 117 944 1478
E: info@kuumba.org.uk
W: www.kuumba.org.uk

Kuumba was founded in 1974 as an Arts and Community Resource Centre in St Paul's, Bristol. Its work includes live events, workshops and participatory activities including dance, music, drama and literature. It works closely with other groups including St Paul's Carnival in Bristol and it coordinates the Afrikan Caribbean Arts Forum.

Live Music Forum
2–4 Cockspur Street
London SW1 5DH
T: 44 (0) 20 7211 6200
E: livemusicforum@culture.gsi.gov.uk

The new Licensing Act of 2003 caused considerable concern among live music presenters and musicians in England and Wales (Scotland is not included under the Act). In February 2004, the Department for Culture, Media and Sport created an ad hoc advisory body to examine the impact the new Act will have on live music. The Forum is composed of a broad range of representatives from the music industry, local government, the arts and venue operators. One of its initiatives is to encourage local authorities (which are the major licensors of live music) to interpret the new laws in a positive and flexible manner that recognises the benefits of live music to the community. In 2006, the Forum will make recommendations to Government (based on a consultation process) for initiatives and further action that will promote the performance of live music in England.

London Musicians' Collective

Unit 3.6
Third Floor, Lafone House
11–13 Leathermarket Street
London SE1 3HN
T: 44 (0) 20 7403 1922
F: 44 (0) 20 7403 1880
E: lmc@lmcltd.demon.co.uk
W: www.l-m-c.org.uk

The London Musicians' Collective is a charity and membership organisation devoted to contemporary music. It promotes improvised and experimental music via concerts and an annual festival. It also runs Resonance FM (see Media: Broadcasting).

Modal

C/o Roots Around the World
The Barn
Fordwater Lane
Chichester
West Sussex PO19 6PT
E: modaluk@btinternet.com

Modal is the only UK organisation drawing together the genres of music falling outside of pop, rock, and classical music. It provides an insight into the vibrant multicultural framework of music existing throughout the UK via an annual three-day convention.

Musicians Union

National Office
60–62 Clapham Road
London SW9 0JJ
T: 44 (0) 20 7582 5566
F: 44 (0) 20 7582 9805
E: info@musiciansunion.org.uk
W: www.musiciansunion.org.uk

Trade Union representing the interests of musicians in all sectors of music. Its website contains information on recommended minimum rates of pay for all types of musicians and for DJ engagements. They also advise on applications for work permits from musicians outside the EU.

National Centre for Early Music

(Please see main entry under Venues and promoters: Yorkshire.)

Performing Arts International Development (PAID)

Creative Industries Division
Department for Culture, Media and Sport
2–4 Cockspur Street
London SW1Y 5DH
T: 44 (0) 20 7211 6296
F: 44 (0) 20 7211 6460
W: www.culture.gov.uk

The PAID Group is one of three industry-led export groups within the Department for Culture, Media and Sport, which brings together government officials and key performing arts trade associations in the creative industries. It identifies arts organisations that might be encouraged to apply for support and assistance through the UK Trade & Investment's (see Statutory agencies) programme of overseas trade exhibitions and seminars, which also offer sources of advice and financial support for export promotion. Other members include the British Council (Statutory agencies), Visiting Arts and AIM (see this section).

Papa Yera
BBC Radio 3 World On Your Street
Photo: Bethan Williams

PRS Foundation for New Music
29–33 Berners Street
London W1T 3AB
T: 44 (0) 20 7306 4044
F: 44 (0) 20 7306 4814
E: info@prsfoundation.co.uk
W: www.prsfoundation.co.uk

Created in 2000, the PRS Foundation is an independent charitable foundation for new music of any genre. The Foundation receives the majority of its funding from the Performing Right Society, which collects licence fees for the public performance and broadcast of musical works. The PRSF gives grants under a number of schemes to UK and non-UK based musicians and composers. Its 'Unsigned' initiative provides support to unsigned acts to be recorded professionally. With the British Council it is funding the 2005 Off-Womex stage in Gateshead.

TAPS (Traditional Arts Projects)
Fairfields Arts Centre
Council Road
Basingstoke
Hampshire RG21 3DH
T: 44 (0) 1256 474014
E: info@tradarts.org
W: www.tradarts.org

Established in 1989 as a folk development agency, TAPS works on intercultural folk projects in the South East of England, although its projects have taken place in most parts of England and it has links with countries such as Chile, India, Finland, Sweden, France and Gambia. TAPS has an extensive schools and lifelong learning programme that involves activities such as drumming, storytelling and song writing. Its One World Band (English, Indian, African, Caribbean and South American musical styles) explores the common ground between cultures, and its RaagHarmonics project enables English and Indian musicians to work together creatively. Boka Halat, a dance and concert band created by TAPS, mixes Gambian rhythm and English melody and includes UK-resident musicians from South Asian, Latin American and Caribbean cultural backgrounds.

Visiting Arts
Bloomsbury House
74–77 Great Russell Street
London WC1B 3DA
T: 44 (0) 20 7291 1601 (information)
F: 44 (0) 20 7291 1616
E: information@visitingarts.org.uk
W: www.visitingarts.org.uk

Visiting Arts advises and assists the UK arts constituency to present high quality contemporary international arts in the UK. It was founded in 1977 as a joint venture between the British Council, Arts Council of Great Britain, the Foreign & Commonwealth Office and the Calouste Gulbenkian Foundation, to increase the flow of foreign arts and artists into the UK. It was made independent of the British Council in 2001 and is now a registered educational charity. Its activities include information, advisory work, professional development and project development (funding and specialist advice). It has a budget of around £1.5 million per annum, two-thirds of which is derived from the Arts Councils of the UK, Foreign & Commonwealth Office, British Council and the Department for Culture, Media and Sport.

It covers nearly all artforms, with a large proportion of its funding supporting the presentation of music from overseas, but it does not support large choirs or orchestras. The Visiting Arts website contains practical information for anyone presenting overseas music or musicians in the UK, whether they are UK-arts practitioners presenting work for the first time or overseas artists keen to make contacts. Their website contains practical information on UK red tape issues such as visas, tax and work permits. Visiting Arts also acts as a useful point of contact for all UK-based cultural attaches, embassies, consulates and cultural institutes.

Wales Arts International (WAI)

Celfyddydau Rhyngwladol Cymru
28 Park Place
Cardiff CF10 3QE
T: 44 (0) 29 2038 3037
F: 44 (0) 29 2039 8778
E: info@wai.org.uk
W: www.wai.org.uk

Wales Arts International was set up in 1997 as a joint venture of the Arts Council of Wales and the British Council Wales to promote international cultural exchange and collaboration between Wales and the world, and covers both export and import of artists and their work. Previous initiatives have included Québec/Cymru, Welsh MCs at the 9th Havana International Hip Hop Festival, and in 2004 it facilitated a group of Welsh organisations to attend Womex 2004 in preparation for Gateshead 2005 (St Donats Arts Centre, Theatr Mwldan, Creu Cymru, the band Fernhill and record label Fflach). They are a good point of contact for information on the international touring opportunities in Wales.

Youth Music

1 America Street
London SE1 0NE
T: 44 (0) 20 7902 1060
F: 44 (0) 20 7902 1061
E: info@youthmusic.org.uk
W: www.youthmusic.org.uk

Youth Music is a UK-wide charity set up in 1999 to provide high quality and diverse music-making opportunities for children aged up to 18. It has several streams of activity:

Youth Music Open Programmes, which are open for general application, target young people living in areas of social and economic need that might otherwise lack opportunity, and predominantly supports activities which are held outside school hours. Funding is available to not-for-profit organisations over a period of six to 24 months. Participants must be 18 or under (or up to 25, with special educational needs [SEN], disabilities or in detention). Music-making activity must take place principally outside school hours (except for children aged up to five and young people with SEN or in detention). There are three schemes: First Steps – creative music-making for children aged up to five; Make It Sound – music-making for 5 to18-year-olds who otherwise lack the chance to take part; and Vocalise! –programmes where the voice is the main instrument.

Partnership Programmes – potential partnership organisations are invited to submit proposals (local authorities, youngchoirs.net etc).

Action Zones – solicited applications from regional consortiums. There are 20 Action Zones – those in England are North East, Humber, North Yorkshire, Greater Manchester, Lancashire, Liverpool and Merseyside, Cumbria, Birmingham, Shropshire and Herefordshire, Staffordshire and Stoke-on-Trent, Corby and Kettering, Lincolnshire, Bristol and Gloucester, Cornwall, Plymouth, Norfolk, Thurrock, Portsmouth and South East Hampshire and London.

Youth Music initiatives – initiatives or events that complement the above programmes such as Songbook (a singing resource), MusicLeader (a professional development scheme) and Cre8 (CD recording project).

Competitions and awards

BBC Radio 3 Awards for World Music
BBC Broadcasting House
Portland Place
London W1A 1AA
T: 44 (0) 20 7580 4468 (main switchboard)
W: www.bbc.co.uk/radio3/awards2005/

(Aka 'The Planets') The UK's major world music award, now in its fourth year. Nominations (made by the public and by delegates to the Womex conference) are in the following categories: Best Artist from Africa, Europe, Americas, Asia/Pacific, Middle East and North Africa, Best Newcomer, Best Boundary Crossing, Club Global, Critics Award and the Audience Award (decided by an online and telephone vote). The winners are selected by a jury; in 2005 they included Youssou N'Dour (Critics Award), Khaled (Middle East and North Africa) and Tinariwen (Africa). The BBC produces a CD with selected tracks by the nominees. The Poll Winners Concert is broadcast on Radio 3, and in 2005 the concert at The Sage Gateshead formed part of a BBC Day of World Music.

BRIT Awards
c/o BPI (British Phonographic Industry)
Riverside Building
County Hall
Westminster Bridge Road
London SE1 7JA
T: 44 (0) 20 7803 1300
E: britawards@jmenternational.com
W: http://brits.co.uk

Created in 1977, the BRITs are promoted by the British Phonographic Industry (see Support bodies) and all proceeds from the broadcast and merchandise from the show go to the BRIT Trust which undertakes projects that enable young people to express their musical creativity. World music is not well represented but previous winners include a number of artists with world music connections such as Björk, Sinead O'Connor, Neneh Cherry, Paul Simon and Peter Gabriel.

Khaled receiving his BBC Radio 3
World Music Award, 2005
(Middle East and North Africa)
Photo: Mark Pinder

MOBO Awards

22 Stephenson Way
London NW1 2HD
T: 44 (0) 20 7419 1800
F: 44 (0) 20 7383 0357
W: www.mobo.com

The MOBOs were created in 1996 to celebrate 'Music Of Black Origin' but the awards now describe themselves as celebrating music from urban culture. MOBO Award categories include R&B, Hip Hop, Reggae, Jazz, Gospel, UK Garage and World Music. A new category will acknowledge musicians from Africa. Winners in the world music category, which was introduced in 2000, include Bebel Gilberto, Santana, Nitin Sawhney, Angelique Kidjo and Ibrahim Ferrer.

Nationwide Mercury Music Prize

W: www.nationwidemercurys.com/

The Mercury Music Prize is a music award given annually for the best British album of the previous 12 months. It was originally sponsored by the telecommunications company Mercury and is now funded by Nationwide Building Society. It is famous for being controversial and diverse in its nominations. The overall winner is chosen from a shortlist of 10 nominees. Nominated artists with world music or culturally diverse music connections include Apache Indian, Courtney Pine, Asian Dub Foundation, Talvin Singh (winner 1999 for *OK*), Nitin Sawhney, Susheela Raman and Eliza Carthy.

URBAN Music Awards

203 Mare Studios
London E8 3QE
T: 44 (0) 870 744 1798
E: info@urbanmusicawards.net
W: www.urbanmusicawards.net

Underground and Urban Music Awards including a category for unsigned acts in Hip Hop, R&B, Soul, Jazz, Blues and Dance.

Denys Baptiste
Let Freedom Ring!
Photo: Rick Guest

Venues and promoters by English region

National touring consortia

Live Roots

T: 44 (0) 1708 377070
E: tonym@salsa.co.uk
W: www.colchesterartscentre.com
C: Tony Morrison, Colchester Roots Club

Live Roots membership comprises Brewery Arts Centre – Kendal; Shrewsbury Buttermarket, Way Art West – Bristol; Colchester Arts Centre, and Band on the Wall – Manchester. It tours reggae, African and Latin music on the small to middle scale. It is an important development structure for emerging artists as well as more established names.

Music Beyond the Mainstream (MBM)

29 New Road
Brighton
East Sussex BN1 1UQ
T: 44 (0) 1273 700747
E: info@brighton-dome.org.uk
W: www.brighton-dome.org.uk
C: Guy Morley

MBM is a consortium of mid-sized (2,000 capacity) venues, which is funded as a circuit by Arts Council England. It offers ready-made tours by jazz, world and roots artists, with four tours a year. The consortium includes St David's Hall (Cardiff), Corn Exchange (Brighton), Usher Hall (Edinburgh), The Anvil (Basingstoke), The Arches (Glasgow), Bridgewater Hall (Manchester), Colston Hall (Bristol), and The Sage Gateshead.

Los de Abajo
Photo: Ricardo Trabulsi/Real World Records

South Asian Music Consortium
85 Duke Street
Liverpool L1 5AP
T: 44 (0) 151 707 1111
F: 44 (0) 151 707 2425
E: info@milapfest.com
W: www.milapfest.com

The South Asian Music Consortium (SAMC) was established in 2001 with the aim of promoting and strengthening South Asian music in the UK. The consortium is a partnership of three leading South Asian arts organisations: Milap Festival Trust – Liverpool; South Asian Arts UK – Leeds, and sampad – Birmingham. Joint projects include retreats, residencies and summer schools, and the South Asian Music Youth Orchestra (SAMYO) and the ensemble Tarang.

East

Arts Development in East
Cambridgeshire (ADeC)
Babylon Gallery
Waterside
Ely
Cambridgeshire CB7 4AU
T: 44 (0) 1353 669022
F: 44 (0) 1353 669052
E: info@adec.org.uk
W: www.adec.org.uk

ADeC aims to promote and support live music in all its forms in the Cambridge district. Its Pop and World Music Development programme includes local concerts of international acts.

Aldeburgh Productions
Snape Maltings Concert Hall
Snape
Suffolk IP17 1SP
T: 44 (0) 1728 687100
F: 44 (0) 1728 687120
E: enquiries@aldeburgh.co.uk
W: www.aldeburgh.co.uk

Aldeburgh Productions is responsible for the Aldeburgh Festival as well as a year-round programme of classical, folk, world music and jazz concerts, opera and contemporary dance, much of which takes place in the main concert hall, the Snape Maltings. Each year the festival and the events programme present a number of world music artists such as Manuel 'Guajiro' Mirabal from Buena Vista Social Club. In addition, Aldeburgh Education and the Britten-Pears Young Artist Programme train young musicians from all over the world. Aldeburgh is one of three international centres of excellence for professional development in music created by Arts Council England in 2003 (Dartington Plus [Hall] and The Sage Gateshead are the other two).

Chakardar
4 Brancaster Drive
Great Notley
Braintree
Essex CM77 7JR
T: 44 (0) 7714 065078
E: harkirat@chakardar.plus.com
W: www.chakardar.com/home_page.htm

Chakardar was established in 1994 as a percussion group to provide students of tabla with opportunities to develop their technical and performance skills. It is now involved in a range of different activities including hosting concerts and recently it launched a series of live recordings. Charkadar runs an annual UK Summer School and brings in tabla masters from India such as Bikram Ghosh, who also appeared at the Rhythm Sticks Festival, South Bank Centre in 2005.

Colchester Arts Centre
Church Street
Colchester
Essex CO1 1NF
T: 44 (0) 1206 500900
F: 44 (0) 1206 500187
E: info@colchesterartscentre.com
W: www.colchesterartscentre.com

The Colchester Arts Centre, which is based in a renovated church, promotes a mixed programme of events including cutting edge and alternative work and up-and-coming pop acts such as The Killers and Athlete. Its world music programme has taken in Salsa Celtica, Merengada and Eduardo Niebla. It is the main point of contact for the Live Roots national consortium.

The hat Factory
65–67 Bute Street
Luton
Bedfordshire LU1 2EY
T: 44 (0) 1582 878100
F: 44 (0) 1582 878109
E: hatfactory@luton.gov.uk
W: www.luton.gov.uk/hatfactory

Opened in 2004, The hat Factory is run by Luton Borough Council and is home to several arts and media organisations, among them the Luton Carnival Arts Development Trust (see Festivals: East). Along with the live music basement venue seating up to 120 people, the Factory also has a Studio Theatre, conference facilities, band rehearsal space, a dance studio and recording studio.

The Junction
Clifton Way
Cambridge CB1 7GX
T: 44 (0) 1223 578000
F: 44 (0) 1223 565600
E: info@junction.co.uk
W: www.junction.co.uk

This large venue in Cambridge (main space, The Stripe, seats 1,050) combines popular rock band and club events with a variety of performing arts, an education and children's programme and the production of new work. Presented artists have included Yat-Kha, Argentinian singer Guillermo Rozenthuler and Koby Israelite. The Junction is also the host of a three-year project called Amplifier, which offers advice to young musicians aged 11–25 on all aspects of the music industry. The Junction is a member of TransEuropeHalles, a European network of 30 venues that offer arts partnership, exchange and training programmes.

Kadam Asian Dance and Music Ltd
1 Lurke Street
Bedford MK40 3TN
T: 44 (0) 1234 316028
E: info@kadam.org.uk
W: www.kadam.org.uk

Kadam is a regional South Asian dance agency, founded in 1991, promoting the appreciation of and participation in South Asian music and dance. It runs a Summer School in partnership with Milap (see Festivals: North West).

Norwich Arts Centre
St Benedicts Street
Norwich NR2 4PG
T: 44 (0) 1603 660387
W: www.norwichartscentre.co.uk

Norwich Arts Centre is based in St Swithin's Church and was redeveloped with the aid of a capital grant from the National Lottery in 1999 (capacity 250 standing). World music events at the venue in 2005 included Yat-Kha, Kroke and Anna Mudeka.

Peppery Productions
45 Corder Road
Ipswich IP4 2XD
E: info@peppery.co.uk
W: www.peppery.co.uk

Promoters based in Ipswich presenting a range of world music in Suffolk, mainly Caribbean and Latin.

East Midlands

Apna Arts
The Art Exchange Gallery
39 Gregory Boulevard
Hyson Green
Nottingham NG7 6BE
T: 44 (0) 115 942 2479
E: info@apnaarts.org.uk
W: www.apnaarts.org.uk

Apna Arts works with South Asian arts (in many genres) nationwide and provides advice, information and advocacy, as well as organising festivals and events. Its music activities focus on young people and club/fusion music and encourage experimentation. Youth projects have involved artists such as Aki Nawaz (of Fun-da-mental) and Bobby Friction. At present it is working in collaboration with other East Midlands organisations to create the New Art Exchange, a new building housing a gallery, exhibition and rehearsal spaces.

Bathysphere
LCB Depot
31 Rutland Street
Leicester LE1 1RE
T: 44 (0) 116 261 6832
F: 44 (0) 116 261 6081
E: info@bathysphere.co.uk
W: www.bathysphere.co.uk

Bathysphere present lo-tempo, chill, ambient and electronica music at various concerts and club events including several European club artists.

China People Promotions
PO Box 6530
Rushden NN10 9ZF
T: 44 (0) 1933 311080
E: info@chinesemusic.co.uk
W: www.chinesemusic.co.uk

China People Promotions (CPP) was formed in 1994 by a group of Chinese musicians. They promote Chinese arts and culture through concerts, festivals, workshops and music production work within the UK and Europe.

De Montfort Hall
Granville Road
Leicester LE1 7RU
T: 44 (0) 116 233 3113
F: 44 (0) 116 233 3182
E: dmh.office@leicester.gov.uk
W: www.demontforthall.co.uk

Leicester's main venue for concerts, the De Montfort Hall (capacity 1,600 seated, 2,200 standing) also hosts a wide range of world music, jazz and roots events. It also has an outdoor amphitheatre (see Summer Sundae, Festivals: East Midlands). Recent artists include Kate Rusby and the African Soul Rebels UK Tour (Daara J, Tinariwen and Rachid Taha).

Lakeside Arts Centre
University Park
Nottingham NG7 2RD
T: 44 (0) 115 846 7777
W: www.lakesidearts.org.uk

Lakeside is part of the University of Nottingham, and is based in Highfields Park. It offers a range of diverse events in all genres. Its music programme includes children's events, classical, world, roots and jazz shows including (recently) Tord Gustavsen's Trio (Norway), Swåp (Sweden/UK) and Malaysian composer Sunetra Fernando. It will be the host for the 2006 Modal meeting (see Support bodies).

The Lift Global Music Club
20 Thorpe Street
Old Glossop
Derbyshire SK13 7RW
T: 44 (0) 1457 862808
E: liftrick@aol.com
W: www.liftglobal.com

The Lift Global Music Club is a non-profit-making organisation run by local volunteers, which presents multicultural music from around the world, and offers workshops in schools and at festivals. Its Global Music Festival 2005 presented Mamadou Cissoko from southern Senegal and guitarist Martin Simpson.

Long Journey Home
W: www.longjourneyhome.org.uk

Long Journey Home began as a region-wide festival in 2002 and has become a network that works with artists in exile and those communities that have recently arrived in the UK, from all over the world, as refugees and asylum seekers. It has regular group meetings and recitals in Nottingham, Derby and Leicester and involves artists from places such as Kurdistan, Iran, the Congo, Angola, Afghanistan, Zimbabwe and the Czech Republic. It organises celebratory music events to mark National Refugee Week and offers training, mentoring, professional development and other support.

Nottingham Asian Arts Council
Nottingham City Council
The Guildhall
South Sherwood Street
Nottingham NG1 4BT
T: 44 (0) 115 915 5555
W: www.nottinghamcity.gov.uk

Based within Nottingham City Council, the Asian Arts Council presents a number of events in the city and beyond and works in partnership with other local organisations to develop and deliver projects.

Phoenix Arts Centre
21 Upper Brown Street
Leicester LE1 5TE
T: 44 (0) 116 224 7700
W: www.phoenix.org.uk

Venue presenting film, theatre, dance and live music. Recent artists include flamenco star Ana de los Reyes.

Royal and Derngate Theatres
Guildhall Road
Northampton NN1 1DP
T: 44 (0) 1604 626222
W: www.royalandderngate.com

The theatres present a range of different musical genres including folk, jazz and world. They are closed for a large capital redevelopment until 2006 and are using local venues in the interim such as the Spinney Hill Theatre. Upcoming acts include Kate Rusby.

Roadmender
1 Ladys Lane
Northampton NN1 3AH
T: 44 (0) 1604 604603
E: operations@roadmender.org
W: www.roadmender.org

Roadmender is Northampton's main live venue for music and performing arts. It presents a wide range of British indie, urban and club music and many international artists such as Congolese Papa Noel and his Afro-Cuban band.

The Y Theatre
7 East Street
Leicester LE1 6EY
T: 44 (0) 116 255 6507
F: 44 (0) 116 255 6509
E: theatre@leicesterymca.co.uk
W: www.leicesterymca.co.uk

Based in the Leicester YMCA (Young Men's Christian Association) The Y Theatre presents a number of world music-oriented nights, usually programming British-based world musicians such as Orquesta Caché and folk artists such as Lynne Heraud and Pat Turner. It also produced a season of world music in Refugee Week 2005.

London

Africa Centre
(See Support bodies).

The Centre presents many African bands.

The Albany
Douglas Way
Depford
London SE8 4AG
T: 44 (0) 20 8692 0231
E: aadmin@thealbany.org.uk
W: www.thealbany.org.uk

Venue in south London, which regularly presents world music.

Asian Dub Foundation Education (ADFED)
Unit 4 Temple Yard
Temple Street
Bethnal Green Road
London E2 6QD
T: 44 (0) 20 7613 4225
F: 44 (0) 20 7613 4192
E: info@adfed.co.uk
W: www.adfed.co.uk

ADFED is the educational wing of British group Asian Dub Foundation. Launched by members of ADF in 1998, ADFED is now an independent project giving training to underrepresented youth communities in the London Borough of Tower Hamlets and the East London region. The organisation is aimed at giving young people who are passionate about making music, opportunities to develop their creativity, especially for those who don't have access to musical equipment and training. It presents music technology workshops and is closely linked to the London Youth Music Action Zone. ADFED will be based at the Rich Mix Centre (a new arts complex which is under construction in the heart of the East End and due to open in 2006).

Barbican Centre
Silk Street
London EC2Y 8DS
T: 44 (0) 20 7638 8891
E: info@barbican.org.uk
W: www.barbican.org.uk

The Barbican is the vast multi-arts and conference centre in the City of London (the largest in Europe.) The Barbican is funded, owned and managed by the Corporation of London and presents a year-round programme of art, music, film and theatre and is home to the Royal Shakespeare Company. It presents and works with a number of promoters and festivals to present world musicians in its concert hall (and in other spaces including its enormous foyer) and has a strong programme of contemporary music festivals. It attracts large capacity audiences and recent notable events include Asha Bhosle, Ali Farke Toure and Paco de Lucia in concert.

Bharatiya Vidya Bhavan (Bhavan Centre)
(See Support bodies.)

Blackheath Halls
23 Lee Road
London SE3 9RQ
T: 44 (0) 20 8318 9758
F: 44 (0) 20 8852 5154
W: www.blackheathhalls.com

The former Blackheath Concert Halls have now been acquired by Trinity College of Music (www.tcm.ac.uk).

Cargo

83 Rivington Street
Kingsland Viaduct
Shoreditch
London EC2A 3AY
T: 44 (0) 20 7749 7840
E: cargomanagers@cantaloupegroup.co.uk
W: www.cargo-london.com

East End bar and club. It presents a wide range of international music and its regular Raison D'Etre night features a number of underground musicians from around the world.

Community Music Ltd (CM)

(See Support bodies.)

Como No

143 Lordship Lane
London SE22 8HX
T: 44 (0) 20 8693 1042
F: 44 (0) 20 8693 6897
E: comono@btinternet.com
W: www.comono.co.uk
C: Andy Wood

Formed in 1986, Como No is a major UK promoter of live Latin music. They have worked with artists such as Veracruz's Mono Blanco, Colombia's Toto La Momposina, Peru's Susan Baca, Omara, Ibrahim, Eliades, Celia Cruz and Wilie Colón, Spanish Harlem Orchestra, the Gotan Project, Kinky and Orishas. Como No habitually promotes in a number of major London venues: Royal Festival Hall, Barbican Centre, Royal Albert Hall, Shepherds Bush Empire, and in clubs, theatres and outdoor events.

Continental Drifts

Unit 1–4 Hilton Grove
Hatherley Mews
London E17 4QP
T: 44 (0) 20 8509 3353
F: 44 (0) 20 8509 9531
info@continentaldrifts.co.uk
www.continentaldrifts.co.uk/htm/driftsfrm.htm

Continental Drifts are (among other things) a music agency and festival creation organisation. They are the largest UK agency for circus/festival acts. They work with a number of festivals as programmers and event coordinators such as the Mayor's Thames Festival, the London Mela and Glastonbury. Their music work began in large-scale percussion projects and now encompasses Desi Remix, Gypsy Dance, Celtic Dance, Ska Cuban, Ska Hip Hop, Celtic Dub, Breakbeat Swingdance and folk punk.

Cultural Co-operation/Music Village

Second Floor
334/336 Goswell Road
London EC1V 7LQ
T: 44 (0) 20 7841 4620
E: info@culturalco-operation.org
W: www.culturalco-operation.org

This London-based cultural organisation, founded (in 1983) and run by Prakash Daswani, is an independent arts charity that promotes cross-cultural contact, dialogue and understanding. It presents the annual Music Village events and maintains the London: Diaspora Capital database (see Media: Websites). The Music Village comprises a large free outdoor event and satellite events and focuses on a range of different cultures every year. Its 2005 Music Village showcased the wealth of London-based world talent.

Cecil Sharp House
2 Regents Park Road
London NW1 7AY
T: 44 (0) 20 7485 2206
F: 44 (0) 20 7284 0534
E: info@efdss.org
W: www.efdss.org/contact.htm

The headquarters of the English Folk Dance and Song Society (see Support bodies) also presents folk, roots and some world music artists.

Darbucka
182 St John Street
Clerkenwell
London EC1 4JZ
T: 44 (0) 20 7490 8772
E: darbuckaecl@yahoo.co.uk
W: www.darbucka.com

The Darbucka restaurant specialises in Arabic and Indian food and holds live world music and dancing events throughout the week.

Emergency Exit Arts
PO Box 570
Greenwich
London SE10 0EE
T: 44 (0) 20 8853 4809
F: 44 (0) 20 8858 2025
E: info@eea.org.uk
W: www.eea.org.uk

EEA, founded in 1980, is a street arts company based in Greenwich producing celebratory events, participatory projects and unusual spectacles. It incorporates the Bollywood Brass Band.

Grand Union
76 Wentworth Street
London E1 7SA
T: 44 (0) 20 7375 1122
F: 44 (0) 20 7426 0268
E: mail@grandunion.org.uk
W: www.grandunion.org.uk/

Created in 1982 Grand Union presents concerts of musicians from all over the world and especially those living in the UK as migrants or as refugees. The Grand Union Orchestra and Grand Union Band (both led by musician Tony Haynes) create and perform new work drawing on the ensemble members own varied cultural and musical backgrounds. Its other activities include professional development, cross-cultural education opportunities and several international projects.

The hub
Unit 10
The Whitechapel Centre
Myrdle Street
London E1 1HL
T: 44 (0) 20 7377 1373
F: 44 (0) 20 7377 1473
E: info@thehubuk.com
W: www.thehubuk.com

The hub is an arts development practice and specialises in business and strategic development, artistic programming and production, fundraising and sponsorship, marketing and brand development, audience development, arts project management and evaluation, and management training. It manages and programmes a number of international music projects, including its 'Fertilizer: Good Shit from...' festivals which have previously focused on Norway and Germany.

Hubble Bubble

45b Myddleton Road
London N22 8LY
T: 44 (0) 7951 167654
E: hubble_bubble@btinternet.com
W: www.hubblebubble.net

Hubble Bubble is an artist-led multicultural platform and presents dancers, live musicians and DJs with a particular emphasis on the music of Turkey and the Southern Mediterranean, Sufi music and dance, and Asian music in its events. Their aim is to create a platform that introduces artists, mostly musicians from different unprivileged ethnic backgrounds, into the market and help to get them out of isolation.

Joyful Noise Music Group

55 Priory Park Rd
London NW6 7UR
T: 44 (0) 20 7328 9613
E: joyfulnoise@talk21.com
W: www.joyfulnoise.co.uk
C: Biyi Adepgba/Barbara Pukwana

Joyful Noise provides organisational support to London-based African and African-Caribbean artists. It also manages, markets and promotes events at the South Bank Centre, Barbican Centre and the Africa Centre. It presents the London African Music Festival which in 2005 joined forces with Africa Remix (part of Africa 2005 – a nationwide festival of African culture,

heritage and arts). Artists appearing at the London African Music Festival included King Sunny Ade, Boubacar Traore, Yvonne Chaka Chaka and a host of African stars.

KAPA Productions

Unit S10B
245a Coldharbour Lane
London SW9 8RR
T: 44 (0) 20 7095 9566
E: info@kapa-productions.com
W: www.kapa-productions.com
C: Katerina Pavlakis

KAPA Productions is an independent organisation promoting 'wonderful music from all corners of the globe' and introducing the best of new, innovative and fascinating artists to audiences across the UK, Europe and beyond. KAPA Productions produces and develops concerts, tours, events and special projects featuring worldwide music and performing arts and undertakes artist management and development.

Kazum!

83 Camelot House
Camden Park Road
London NW1 9AS
T: 44 (0) 20 7267 7445
E: info@kazum.co.uk
W: www.kazum.co.uk

Kazum! (which is the reverse of 'muzak') are live music and tour producers. Their productions have included Balkan gypsy bands, Italian tarantella, Argentinian tango songs, Madagascan guitar, Turkish folk music, Sufi-electronica, and Istanbul club nights.

Momo

25–27 Heddon Street
London W1B 4BH
T: 44 (0) 20 7434 4040

London restaurant with a North African menu which presents world music on a regular basis.

Notting Hill Arts Club

21 Notting Hill Gate
London W11 3JQ
T: 44 (0) 20 7460 4459
E: david@nottinghillartsclub.com
W: www.nottinghillartsclub.com

This small capacity venue is home to a number of independently promoted club events, such as Martin Morales' *Futuro Flamenco*, Patrick Forge's *Brazilian Love Affair* and Bobby Friction and Nihal's *Bombay Bronx*.

South Asian Music Youth
Orchestra (SAMYO) in concert
Photo: Vipul Sangoi, Raindesign

Serious
Chapel House
18 Hatton Place
London EC1N 8RU
T: 44 (0) 20 7405 9900
F: 44 (0) 20 7405 9911
E: info@serious.org.uk
W: www.serious.org.uk

(See also Agents and managers). Serious is an international producer of jazz, world and contemporary music and promotes widely throughout London, the UK and internationally, often working with the larger London venues such as the Barbican and Queen Elizabeth Hall. Recent presentations have included Paco de Lucia, Vusi Mahlasela and Jamie Cullum. They are the promoters of the international London Jazz Festival (see Festivals: London). Their publishing arm, In All Seriousness Music, is a new venture with Big Life Music Publishing.

School of Oriental and African Studies (SOAS)
University of London
Thornhaugh Street
Russell Square
London WC1H 0XG
T: 44 (0) 20 7637 2388
F: 44 (0) 20 7436 3844
W: www.soas.ac.uk

SOAS is a major centre for ethnomusicology research and performance and incorporates the AHRB Research Centre for Cross-Cultural Music and Dance Performance. This centre aims to promote, coordinate, and disseminate research on cross-cultural performance with particular reference to Asian and African traditions. SOAS is a venue for cultural festivals, such as Klez Fest, and there are often recitals of music in its striking Brunei Gallery.

The Shrine
c/o Musicians Incorporated
45 Harcourt Road
London N22 7XW
T: 44 (0) 20 8888 1064
F: 44 (0) 20 8888 1026
E: info@musiciansincorporated.com
W: www.theshrine.uk.com

Created by Rita Ray and Max Reinhardt, The Shrine was named after Fela Kuti's club in Lagos and is dedicated to afrobeat. The Shrine Synchro System, described as a 'specially deconstructed version of a Shrine club session' has toured to Uganda, Lithuania, Estonia, Slovenia, Bulgaria, Romania, Poland, Finland, Russia and the Ukraine.

South Bank Centre
Belvedere Road
London SE1 8XX
T: 44 (0) 20 7921 0600
W: www.southbankcentre.org.uk

The South Bank Centre is a collection of venues and galleries on the South Bank of the Thames near Waterloo Railway Station. The largest performance venue is the Royal National Theatre which offers free live music in its foyer most days of the week, and in summer this takes place outside – quite a number of the bands are folk, roots or world oriented.

The large concert hall, the Royal Festival Hall (RFH) was originally built as a temporary hall for the Festival of Britain in 1951. The RFH is an orchestral venue but has an eclectic programme which includes major world music stars such as Tony Allen (with UK urban music star Dizzee Rascal). The large foyer space also serves as an informal performance space and there is free music (often by international artists) before the main concert events in the hall. (The RFH will be closed for refurbishment from 2005 and there will be a large scale revamp of the whole South Bank Centre site.)

The Queen Elizabeth Hall (QEH), which is the next largest, offers a wide range of different events, including many outside hires by cultural organisations. Recent appearances include Boubacar Traore, Yvonne Chaka Chaka and Eliza Carthy. The Purcell Room, which is adjacent to the QEH, is a recital venue and suits smaller ensembles: again the programming is wide-ranging and the space is frequently the setting for Asian, African and Latin artists such as Rachel Magoola from Uganda.

The South Bank Centre plays host to several important events: the Rhythm Sticks Festival, Meltdown, La Linea Latin Festival, the London International Jazz Festival, and many smaller but exciting programmes of international music.

The Spitz

109 Commercial Street
Old Spitalfields Market
London E1 6BG
T: 44 (0) 20 7247 9747
E: mail@spitz.co.uk
W: www.spitz.co.uk

The Spitz is a project of The Dandelion Trust, an organisation which supports the arts, helps people in traumatic situations and conserves green spaces and beautiful buildings. The Spitz is part of the Spitalfields Market regeneration project and comprises a gallery, a bar-restaurant and a performance space. The performance programme is a regular date on the world music touring circuit and The Spitz has presented some of the most well-known world music stars over the years. Its recent events include the Spitz Festival of Folk, Susheela Raman, Japanese-Brazilian band Ohayo Samba and the Grand Union Bangla Band.

YaD Arts

Suite 49
Basildon Court
28 Devonshire Street
London W1G 6PR
T: 44 (0) 20 7535 0251
E: info@yadarts.com
W: www.yadarts.com

YaD Arts place modern Jewish culture alongside the myriad influences of a contemporary, multicultural society, and they work with a number of art genres including music. They strive to present, in positive ways, the experience of the majority of young people growing up in an urban society with multi-faceted cultural identities. YaD Arts represents over 30 artists and musicians both nationally and internationally as agents, supporting their work, as well as their tours, at music festivals and venues worldwide. Their roster includes Oi Va Voi. Their other work includes education and outreach, events organisation, event programming and artist support.

Watermans Arts Centre

40 High Street
Brentford TW8 0DS
T: 44 (0) 20 8232 1020
F: 44 (0) 20 8232 1030
W: www.watermans.org.uk

The Watermans is a major arts centre in West London presenting (among other work) Asian theatre, dance and music.

North East

Alnwick Playhouse
Bondgate Without
Northumberland NE66 1PQ
T: 44 (0) 1665 510785
F: 44 (0) 1665 605962
E: info@alnwickplayhouse.co.uk
W: www.alnwickplayhouse.co.uk

Based in a former 1920s cinema, the Playhouse presents a programme of music (world and folk), drama, dance, film and exhibitions.

Arc
Dovecot Street
Stockton on Tees TS18 1LL
T: 44 (0) 1642 525180
E: info@arconline.co.uk
W: www.arconline.co.uk

Arts Centre comprising a theatre, studio, gallery and other spaces which programme a mix of musics, including some folk and world.

Darlington Arts Centre
Vane Terrace
Darlington DL3 7AX
T: 44 (0) 1325 348843
E: info@darlingtonarts.co.uk
W: www.darlingtonarts.co.uk

Large venue in a multi-purpose arts centre programming jazz, Latin, R&B and folk music.

Folkworks
(See The Sage Gateshead in this section.)

Jumpin' Hot Club
Live Theatre
Quayside
Newcastle upon Tyne NE1 3DQ
T: 44 (0) 191 232 1232
E: info@jumpinhot.com
W: www.jumpinhot.com

Primarily a blues and roots venue, the Jumpin' Hot Club has been in existence for over 20 years and presents rockabilly, ska, country, rock and roll, reggae, world music and jazz. One of its earliest artists was Boubacar Traore. It also operates a second venue at The Cluny in Byker, and promotes gigs across the region as well as the festival Northern Roots.

Kalapremi
21 Beamish View
Stanley
County Durham DH9 OXB
T: 44 (0) 1207 290606
E: contact@kalapremi.org

Kalapremi organise the Ganesh Festival at the LampLight Arts Centre, an annual celebration of cultural diversity and the arts which includes Chinese and Afro-Caribbean performers as well as Indian artists.

LampLight Arts Centre
Front Street
Stanley
County Durham DH9 0NA
T: 44 (0) 1207 218899
F: 44 (0) 1207 218897
E: lamplight@derwentside.gov.uk
W: www.derwentside.gov.uk

Arts Centre with a capacity of 430 (seated) operated by the local authority. Seckou Keita has performed here.

The Sage Gateshead
PO Box 254
Gateshead NE8 2YR
T: 44 (0) 191 443 4666
F: 44 (0) 191 443 4550
W: www.thesagegateshead.org

The Sage Gateshead is an arresting £70 million new building, situated on the quayside in Gateshead, designed by Norman Foster and owned by Gateshead Council who commissioned it. The North Music Trust, which operates the building, is the result of an unprecedented collaboration of a chamber orchestra, the Northern Sinfonia, and the folk agency Folkworks, to create a programme of acoustic, indie, country, world, folk, jazz, electronic, dance and classical music. Apart from its two main auditoria, which both have excellent acoustics, the building includes a large concourse, several other smaller spaces and a 25-room Music Education Centre, which forms, literally, the foundations on which the building sits. (The Sage offers a degree in Folk and Traditional Music).

Its world music programme is extensive and was the host for the Poll Winners Party of the 2005 BBC Awards for World Music starring (among others) Khaled and Tinariwen. It is the host of the 2005 Womex. The Sage is also one of the three international centres of excellence for professional development in music created by Arts Council England in 2003 (Dartington Plus (Hall) and Aldeburgh are the other two).

North West

Band on the Wall
c/o Inner City Music
25 Swan Street
Manchester M4 5JZ
E: project@bandonthewall.org
W: www.bandonthewall.org

Band on the Wall is a long-standing music venue with an international reputation based in a public house. It got its name because the performance stage was situated halfway up the wall over the heads of the audience. It is currently undergoing a renovation and will be closed until 2007.

Brewery Arts Centre
122a Highgate
Kendal
Cumbria LA9 4HE
T: 44 (0) 1539 725133
F: 44 (0) 1539 730257
E: admin@breweryarts.co.uk
W: www.breweryarts.co.uk

Arts Centre with a 350 capacity (seated) music space. Recent artists include Dennis Rollins and North Stars Steel Orchestra, Robert Maseko and Congobeat, Transglobal Underground, and Mabulu from Mozambique.

Bridgewater Hall

The Bridgewater Hall
Lower Mosley Street
Manchester M2 3WS
T: 44 (0) 161 950 0000
F: 44 (0) 161 950 0001
E: admin@bridgewater-hall.co.uk
W: www.bridgewater-hall.co.uk

The Hall is a major concert venue in Manchester, based in an award-winning new building which opened in 1996. It programmes all genres of music and recent jazz/world artists have included Wynton Marsalis, the Master Drummers of Africa and flamenco master Juan Martin.

Lowry Centre

The Lowry
Pier 8
Salford Quays M50 3AZ
T: 44 (0) 870 787 5780
F: 44 (0) 161 876 2001
E: info@thelowry.com
W: www.thelowry.com

The Lowry forms one of the key pieces of the redeveloped Salford Quays in Greater Manchester. It presents a big programme of jazz, folk and world music and also runs a programme of Asian music and dance.

More Music in Morecambe

The Hothouse
13–17 Devonshire Road
Morecambe LA3 1QS
T: 44 (0) 1524 831997
F: 44 (0) 1524 419653
E: info@mormusic.net
W: www.mormusic.net

MMM is a community music development agency working regionally and nationally to increase participation in music-making among the young and all ages. MMM manages the Youth Music Action Zone for the county, a South Asian music group for young people – Dhamak: Asian Beats (covering DJs, dhol drumming and rapping skills) and a number of musical training and education classes and events. They also present events in the Hothouse venue where they are based and at jazz, folk and world music festivals.

Multi Asian Arts Centre

129 Drake Street
Rochdale OL16 1PZ
T: 44 (0) 1706 642954
E: maac@btconnect.com
W: www.users.zetnet.co.uk/maac

MAAC is a voluntary community Asian arts development organisation formed in 1987 and through Edexcel (the largest qualifications awarding body in the UK) and Greater Manchester Open College Network, it is an accredited training centre in Asian arts (BTEC). MAAC coordinates, promotes and develops Asian arts throughout the region in collaboration with local authorities, arts organisations, schools, community centres and individual artists, helping to devise, plan and organise annual events, festivals (Melas), projects, tours and other art-related activities. It also answers many general enquiries and maintains a database of local freelance Asian artists. In 2002 it began a collaboration with the Alhamra Arts Council, Lahore, Pakistan.

Royal Liverpool Philharmonic Hall
Hope Street
Liverpool
Merseyside L1 9BP
T: 44 (0) 151 709 2895
T: 44 (0) 151 210 2902
E: info@liverpoolphil.com
W: www.liverpoolphil.com

The Philharmonic Hall has been a cultural landmark in Liverpool since 1849. It is home to the Royal Liverpool Philharmonic Orchestra and it has also presented concerts by The Beatles and The Rolling Stones. Its world music programme is strong and includes an ongoing collaboration with Asian arts organisation Milap (see Festivals: North West) including a concert with Anoushkar Shankar. Recent artists presented include Nitin Sahwney, Ravi Shankar, Oumou Sangaré and Idrissa Soumaoro.

South East

The Anvil
Churchill Way
Basingstoke
Hampshire RG21 7QR
T: 44 (0) 1256 819 797
F: 44 (0) 1256 331 733
E: box.office@theanvil.org.uk
W: www.theanvil.org.uk

A large music venue in Basingstoke presenting many genres of music. Its folk, jazz and world music programme has included Ladysmith Black Mambazo, Vusi Mahlasela and Kate Rusby. Alongside its public events, The Anvil runs a community and education programme.

Brighton Dome
29 New Road
Brighton
East Sussex BN1 1UQ
T: 44 (0) 1273 700747
E: info@brighton-dome.org.uk
W: www.brighton-dome.org.uk

The Dome consists of three spaces: the Concert Hall, the Corn Exchange and the Pavilion Theatre. The Concert Hall has recently undergone a lottery-funded rebuilding and refurbishment programme and has a maximum capacity of 1,872 (seated). Its programme has included many top names in folk, world and pop including Spanish Harlem Orchestra, Mariza, and Asian Dub Foundation.

Komedia Brighton
44 Gardner Street
Brighton BN1 1UN
T: 44 (0) 1273 647101
E: admin@komedia.co.uk
W: www.komedia.co.uk

Komedia is a cabaret, comedy, theatre and music venue putting on around 700 international and national events annually in its three spaces. It runs a summer world music programme called Globalista, and presents many world artists throughout the year. Recent appearances have been made by Yat-Kha, Los de Abajo (Mexico), Transglobal Underground and Manu Chao's proteges Go Lem System (Spain).

Music for Change

19b Roper Close
Canterbury
Kent CT2 7EP
T: 44 (0) 1227 459243
E: info@musicforchange.org
W: www.musicforchange.org

Music for Change (founded in 1997) is an arts organisation that promotes understanding and respect for cultural diversity through music. Its core work involves organising workshops (one-offs and residencies), mainly in schools, with a strong emphasis on creativity and confidence building in the classroom. It also produces the Global Weekend in Canterbury in November and Safe and Sound, a two-year refugee project, focusing on the theme of migration.

Oxford Contemporary Music

Westminster Institute of Education
Harcourt Hill
Oxford OX2 9AT
T: 44 (0) 1865 488369
F: 44 (0) 1865 488317
E: info@ocmevents.org
W: www.ocmevents.org

Oxford Contemporary Music is one of the leading new music promoters in the south of England. They promote over 30 events each year. Their programme includes world music presentations and their 2005 season focuses on the music of the Baltic states. Other artists presented by them have included the Mostar Sevdah Reunion, Jaly Fily Cissokho from Senegal and Tunisian oud player Dhafer Youssef.

Roots Around the World

The Barn
Fordwater Lane
Chichester
West Sussex PO19 6PT
T: 44 (0) 1243 789786
F: 44 (0) 1243 789787
E: markringwood@btinternet.com
W: www.rootsaroundtheworld.info

Roots Around the World is run by Mark and Sue Ringwood who seek to promote a better understanding of cultural diversity by staging concerts, workshops and festivals primarily in West Sussex, Surrey, and Hampshire. The organisation embraces what used to be the mARKO pOLO agency and frequently organises national tours for artists, and international festival engagements. Mark Ringwood presents a radio show *Roots Around the World* broadcast every Sunday 7–10pm on Spirit FM (www.spiritfm.net).

Turner Sims Concert Hall

University of Southampton
Highfield Road
Southampton SO17 1BJ
T: 44 (0) 23 8059 2223
F: 44 (0) 23 8059 2505
E: info@turnersims.co.uk
W: www.artsline.co.uk/ts

Based at the University of Southampton, the Turner Sims Concert Hall seats 460. Recent artists have included Tunisian oud player Dhafer Youssef, Cuba's Vocal Sampling, Chango Spasiuk, Raga Nova (Dharambir Singh [sitar] and Jesse Bannister [saxophone]), and programmes such as Shaman Voices which presented Mongolian shaman Okna Tsahan Zam alongside Wimme Saari, a joik singer from Finland.

South West

Colston Hall
Colston Street
Bristol BS1 5AR
T: 44 (0) 117 922 3686
E: boxoffice@colstonhall.org
W: www.colstonhall.org

Colston Hall is the South West's largest concert venue. It will shortly undergo a large lottery-funded revamp. Its programme covers classic music, jazz, rock, world and folk.

DartingtonARTS
Higher Close
Dartington
Totnes
Devon TQ9 6DE
T: 44 (0) 1803 847070
W: www.dartingtonarts.org.uk

Based in the Dartington Hall estate and adjacent to the Dartington College of Arts, DartingtonARTS runs a year-round programme of music, dance and contemporary performance, theatre and film. It is also the venue for the Dartington International Summer School. The Dartington Hall Trust, Dartington College of Arts and King Edward VI Community College make up Dartington Plus, one of three international centres of excellence for professional development in music created by Arts Council England in 2003 (The Sage Gateshead and Aldeburgh are the other two). Dartington Plus recently formed a partnership with the WOMAD Foundation to create *Africa and Beyond: Cultural Connections*.

Eden Project
Bodelva
St Austell
Cornwall 2SG PL24
T: 44 (0) 1726 811911
F: 44 (0) 1726 811912
W: www.edenproject.com

The strange, space-age 'biomes' of the Eden Project are now a Cornish icon. They contain 'the world's biggest jungle in captivity'. Created by Tim Smit to mark the year 2000, it is a 'Living Theatre of Plants and People'. Eden runs a number of live music events inside and outside the biomes, most notably the recent LIVE 8 Africa Calling Concert in July 2005 (put together by WOMAD). Eden is a regular host to world musicians. Their 2005 Jungle Nights programme, for example, included Congolese/Ugandan group Zambula and Zimbabweans Chimanimani. The Eden Sessions featuring mainstream international and British pop acts have also become extremely popular: the 2005 season includes Keane, Embrace, Basement Jaxx and Ian Brown of the Stone Roses.

Kuumba
(See Support bodies.)

St George's Bristol
Great George Street
off Park Street
Bristol BS1 5RR
T: 44 (0) 117 923 0359
F: 44 (0) 117 927 6537
E: boxoffice@stgeorgesbristol.co.uk
W: www.stgeorgesbristol.co.uk

This chamber music venue, which also programmes world and jazz, is well known for its acoustics and underwent a large capital rebuild in 1999.

Lighthouse
Kingland Road
Poole
Dorset BH15 1UG
T: 44 (0) 1202 665334
F: 44 (0) 1202 670016
E: website@lighthousepoole.co.uk
W: www.lighthousepoole.co.uk/

Based in Poole, the Lighthouse underwent a large lottery-funded rebuild in 2002. It is now the largest arts centre outside London with a 669-seat theatre, 1,500-seat concert hall, 150-seat studio and 105-seat cinema. The world music programme has included Nitin Sawhney, Orchestra Baobab, Susana Baca, Lila Downs, Yusa, Taj Mahal and Idrissa Soumaoro, Stella Chiweshe and the African Soul Rebels UK Tour (Rachid Taha, Tinariwen and Daara J).

Way Art West
(See Cactus Jazz in Agents and managers.)

West Midlands

Birmingham Jazz
19 Selwyn Road
Edgbaston
Birmingham B16 0SH
T: 44 (0) 121 454 2371
W: www.birminghamjazz.co.uk

Birmingham Jazz promotes contemporary jazz in the city. It is a voluntary organisation but engages freelance consultants on larger projects. It promotes up to 35 concerts a year in various venues including the CBSO Centre, the mac (Midland Arts Centre), the Adrian Boult Hall etc. It has also promoted at The Drum, The Custard Factory and the Sanctuary Night Club. International musicians feature in its regular programming and commissioning activities including such artists as The African Allstars and Tord Gustavsen Trio.

Black Voices
23 Sherwood Gardens
Catlin Street
Rotherhithe
London SE16 3JA
T: 44 (0) 121 441 1421
F: 44 (0) 121 441 2568
W: www.blackvoices.co.uk

Black Voices was founded in 1987 and aims to re-present Black music from a Caribbean, Black British perspective, particularly sacred and secular a cappella and gospel. They present The A cappella Festival at The Drum. Supported by Arts Council England and others, Black Voices is also developing a range of creative opportunities in music and music technology from a centre in Birmingham. CMAT (Centre for Music and Arts Technology) in

Handsworth will act as a 'one stop' resource and facility centre for musicians and will encourage young people to become engaged in a cappella.

The Buttermarket/Jazz and Roots Club
74 Copthorne Drive
Shrewsbury SY3 8RX
T: 44 (0) 1743 231142
W: www.buttermarket.com/buttermarket
W: www.jazzandroots.com/jazzandroots

Since the mid-1980s, when it presented early pioneers like Bhundu Boys, the Jazz and Roots Club presents jazz, world, folk and roots acts on a regular weekly basis, plus some rock and indie bands. It has become the UK's longest-running specialist Roots/World Music Club, and is based at The Buttermarket. Recent appearances have been made by Kekele, Tony Allen, Capercaille, Wayne Gorbea and Dennis Rollins. It is part of the Live Roots Network.

The Custard Factory
Gibb Square
Birmingham B9 4AA
T: 44 (0) 121 224 7777
E: info@custardfactory.com
W: www.custardfactory.com

Birmingham's new arts and media quarter is housed in the former Bird's Custard Factory, a five-acre (two hectares) site in the centre of the city and incorporates studios for 500 artists and small creative enterprises, The Medicine Bar and the Code nightclub. The Medicine Bar programmes world-oriented DJ nights and live acts such as Martin Morales' Shaanti and Norman Jay.

The Drum
144 Potters Lane
Aston
Birmingham B6 4UU
T: 44 (0) 121 333 2400
F: 44 (0) 121 333 2440
E: info@the-drum.org.uk
W: www.the-drum.org.uk

The Drum is a Birmingham-based, multi-purpose arts centre dedicated to the development and promotion of African, Asian and Caribbean arts. Its recent Diaspora series brought world music groups to the venue including Smadj and Dele Sosimi's Afrobeat Orchestra. Aside from this The Drum regularly presents musicians from around the world including The African Jazz Allstars, Julian Marley and Qawwali star Qari Waheed Chishti.

mac (Midlands Arts Centre)
Cannon Hill Park
Birmingham B12 9QH
T: 44 (0) 121 440 3838
E: info@macarts.co.uk
W: www.macarts.co.uk

mac is one of the busiest arts centres in Britain and presents a strong programme of music, both in-house promotions and with external promoters such as sampad. Recent visitors include Yat-Kha, Jaleo Flamenco and Oswin Chin Behilia from the Dutch Antilles.

Sounds In The Round is a summer festival programme which runs at weekends in mac's open air arena. Highlights have included Olodum, Oumou Sangare and Kathryn Tickell. It is produced in association with World Unlimited (see later in this section).

sampad (South Asian Arts)
c/o mac
Cannon Hill Park
Birmingham B12 9QH
T: 44 (0) 121 446 4312
F: 44 (0) 121 440 8667
E: info@sampad.org.uk
W: www.sampad.org.uk

sampad is an arts development agency for South Asian Arts based in Birmingham. Music is one of the key strands of sampad's work and it has a number of initiatives to encourage participation in South Asian music. Along with Milap and SAA-uk it has formed the South Asian Music Consortium (SAMC), (see Venues and promoters: National consortia) and the SAMYO orchestra and the Tarang Ensemble. Its educational work includes projects which promote collaborations between Asian and African musicians, such as its Africasia. sampad works in partnership with many local and national organisations and regularly presents showcases at mac (Midlands Arts Centre, where it is based) and other venues.

Sound It Out
The Arch
Unit G9, 48–52 Floodgate Street
Birmingham B5 5SL
T: 44 (0) 121 773 7322
F: 44 (0) 121 773 1117
E: enquiries@sounditout.co.uk
W: www.sounditout.co.uk

Sound It Out is a development agency for innovative participatory music and employs professional musicians to work with people with any level of musical experience or none at all to create and perform music throughout Birmingham and beyond. It works with schools, young people, refugees, local authorities and venues in a range of different musical styles.

Surdhwani
3 Sherington Drive
Goldthorn Park
Wolverhampton WV4 5DX
T: 44 (0) 1902 658 793
F: 44 (0) 1902 830 278
E: sarcar@surdhwani.org.uk
W: surdhwani.org.uk

Surdhwani brings the great masters of Indian classical music and dance to perform in Wolverhampton and the surrounding region of 'The Black Country' and runs music and dance classes in vocal, tabla and Kathak dance.

Warwick Arts Centre
University of Warwick
Coventry CV4 7AL
T: 44 (0) 24 7652 4524
W: www.wawickartscentre.co.uk

Warwick Arts Centre in Coventry is the largest arts centre in the Midlands, attracting around 280,000 visitors a year to over 2,000 individual events embracing music, drama, dance, comedy, literature, films and visual art. Recent world, folk and roots stars to have appeared there include Kate Rusby, Mariza and Pink Martini.

World Unlimited
W: www.worldunlimited.freeuk.com

World Unlimited is a voluntary, not-for-profit, organisation formed in 1989 to bring the best in international roots artists to Birmingham including Angelique Kidjo, Yusa, Taj Mahal, Kate Rusby, Rizwan-Muazzam Qawwali, The Wailers and Ananda Shankar.

Yorkshire

Juju Club
84 Stag Works
John Street
Sheffield S2 4QU
T: 44 (0) 114 249 6557
E: info@jujuclub.co.uk
W: www.jujuclub.co.uk
C: Alan Deadman

Popular Sheffield club programming global dance and world music acts such as Hugh Masekela, Kanda Bongo Man, Misty and Roots, Fun-da-mental, Jesus Alemany, Roberto Pla, Mouth Music and Shooglenifty. The Juju works in close collaboration with monthly club Headcharge, which plays acid techno trance, dub, reggae, drum and bass and break beat.

National Centre for Early Music
St Margaret's Church
Walmgate
York Y01 9TL
T: 44 (0) 1904 632220
F: 44 (0) 1904 612631
E: info@ncem.co.uk
W: www.ncem.co.uk

NCEM is based in St Margaret's Church, York, which is also home to the York Early Music Festival and the Beverley and East Riding Early Music Festival. The Centre presents many jazz, folk and world musicians within its World Sounds programme and curates a number of themed festivals and seasons of work, such as The African Music Festival Weekend in 2005 which included the Tuareg group, Ensemble Tartit. York has a sizeable Chinese population and the NCEM produces a Chinese New Year event which is also funded by the urban regeneration programme of the city council.

South Asian Arts UK (SAA-uk)
3 St Peters Buildings
St Peters Square
Leeds LS9 8AH
T: 44 (0) 113 244 5523
F: 44 (0) 113 244 1319
E: info@saa-uk.org.uk
W: www.saa-uk.org.uk

SAA-uk was founded in 1997 with the help of the Leeds College of Music and National Lottery funding. It works with a number of artforms with the focus on music (from throughout the Asian subcontinent and hybrid British-Asian artforms). Its activities include residencies for musicians from India, schools and community workshops, performances and outreach work. Its Raga Muffins Project is aimed at 8 to 18-year-olds and creates open access opportunities for young people to engage in South Asian music-making in the school holidays, through intensive musical residencies, led by experienced Asian classical musicians in sitar, santoor, tabla and voice. It is a member of the South Asian Music Consortium (see National touring consortia in this section).

Agents and managers

Access All Areas
44 Alexandra Avenue
Meole Brace
Shrewsbury SY3 9HS
T: 44 (0) 1743 235384
E: accessallareas@btinternet.com
W: www.accessallareas.info

Access All Areas represents international artists from the Roots and World scene. Their roster includes the Jaipur Kawa Brass Band, Kekele, Achanak, The Baghdaddies and Bayou Seco. They organise UK tours and manage bookings for a number of UK-based acts.

Adastra
2 Star Row
North Dalton
Driffield
East Yorkshire YO25 9UX
T: 44 (0) 1377 217 662
F: 44 (0) 1377 217 754
E: adastra@adastra-music.co.uk
W: www.adastra-music.co.uk
C: Chris Wade

Adastra is one of the UK's leading agencies specialising in folk, roots, world and acoustic music. The agency was established in 1988 in the North of England. It works with artists from Britain and around the world organising concerts, tours and workshops. Artists include the Unusual Suspects from Scotland, La Bottine Souriante from Québec, Lúnasa, Danu and Eleanor McEvoy from Ireland, Black Umfolosi from Zimbabwe, the Warsaw Village Band from Poland and Martin Simpson from England. The agency is also involved in various projects including the promoters' network Nu Routes, and the Beverley and East Riding Folk Festival.

African & Caribbean Music Circuit
(See Support bodies.)

Buena Vista Social Club,
World Circuit Records, 1997
Photo: Geraint Lewis

Apartment 22

19 Tewkesbury Road
Bristol BS2 9UL
T: 44 (0) 117 955 6615
E: andy.morgan@apartment22.com

Apartment 22 and Andy Morgan have been managing Tinariwen since 2001 having met them at the first Festival in the Desert, in January of that year. Apartment 22 had previously been a small label specialising in global electronica but have since consolidated their activities to concentrate on organising the tours, records and merchandising for the very busy and successful Tinariwen.

Asian Music Circuit

Ground Floor
Unit E, West Point
33/34 Warple Way
London W3 0RG
T: 44 (0) 20 8742 9911
F: 44 (0) 20 8749 3948
E: info@amc.org.uk
W: www.amc.org.uk

(See the main entry in Support bodies.) The Asian Music Circuit promotes tour concerts and educational projects and aims to bring the best of traditional and contemporary music, reflecting living traditions from Asia, to the widest public possible. The AMC manages artists from Central Asia to Indonesia but especially from South Asia. It also supports and gives advice to Asian artists based in the UK.

Cactus Jazz/Way Art West

14 Westbourne Road
Easton
Bristol BS1 5AR
T: 44 (0) 117 902 5079
E: info@cactujazz.co.uk
W: www.cactusjazz.co.uk
E: info@wawagency.com
W: www.wawagency.com
C: Paul Fordham

With involvement in concert promotion, touring (including touring consortia) and consultancy for more than 10 years, this company has a long experience in world and diverse music in Britain. Way Art West has introduced some of the most promising new artists from Africa to the UK including Manecas Costa in 2001 and Lura in 2003. 2005 sees the development of this experience into a new touring agency called WAW agency.

Coda Agency

Second Floor
81 Rivington Street
London EC2A 3AY
T: 44 (0) 20 7012 1555
F: 44 (0) 20 7012 1566
E: agents@codaagency.com
W: www.codaagency.com
C: Rob Challice

International agency and tour producer. They work predominantly with dance, pop, rock, jazz, have a sizeable roster and specialist knowledge of world music. Rob Challice is the company's world music expert and represents artists such as Yat-Kha, King Sunny Ade, Denys Baptiste, and Jazz Jamaica.

C7M World

47 Whitehall Park
London N19 3TW
T: 44 (0) 20 7272 4413
F: 44 (0) 20 7281 9687
E: admin@c7m.co.uk
W: www.c7m.co.uk

C7M (or Clarion Seven Muses) manages a number of world music tours every year including Fanfare Ciocarlia, The Gnawa Bop Experience, Katia Guerreiro, Varttina and Jony Iliev and Band.

Dug Up Music

22 Hill Street
Reading RG1 2NU
T: 44 (0) 7855 253 457
E: hope@dugupmusic.com
W: www.dugupmusic.com
C: Hope Cooper

Dug Up Music offers management and music production for musicians worldwide as well as programming and promoting innovative roots/world music events primarily in the UK. Seeking out new and exciting musical talent from far flung corners of the globe, Dug Up Music aims to broaden artists' horizons by enabling them to travel and perform overseas while bringing audiences together in a greater appreciation of our cultural diversity.

Elastic Artists Agency Ltd

No 5
3 Newhams Road
London SE1 3UZ
T: 44 (0) 20 7367 6224
F: 44 (0) 20 7367 6206
E: info@elasticartists.net
W: www.elasticartists.net
C: Jon Slade

A young London-based agency dealing with the full range of live music and DJs. From rock to world via jazz, hip hop and electronica, they have an interesting roster of world music artists from traditionally-based acts to world-influenced DJs including Bembe Segue, Jaga Jazzist, Talvin Singh, Punjabi MC and Hit Squad, and Oi Va Voi.

Far Side Music

80c Belsize Park Gardens
London NW3 4NG
T: 44 (0) 20 7722 3054
E: mail@farsidemusic.com
W: www.farsidemusic.com
C: Paul Fisher

Far Side Music manages internationally several Japanese and Asian artists, promoting their music in the UK and overseas, by arranging record releases, festival appearances and tours. They also license, export and promote other 'world music' into Japan and other Asian countries. (See also Labels and distributors.)

Frusion
1 Holme Road
Matlock Bath
Derbyshire DE4 3NU
T: 44 (0) 1629 57082
E: info@frusion.co.uk
W: www.frusion.co.uk
C: Ian Smith

Frusion is an independent agency that promotes collaborations between artists worldwide, from Argentina to France, to America, the Balkans, North Africa, Asia and the UK. They also work with DJs and VJs. They specialise in new musical projects and handle new talent across a broad range of world and folk dance music. Current artists include Joi, The Angel Brothers, Xosé Manuel Budiño, La Chicana, Dissidenten, Martin Morales and Oojami. Frusion is run and owned by Ian Smith, a Musicians Union member for many years, and currently chair of the national committee of the Musicians Union, Folk, Roots and Traditional Music section.

ICM

4–6 Soho Square
London W1D 3PZ
T: 44 (0) 20 7432 0800
E: jazzworld@icmtalent.com
W: www.icmtalent.com

Jazz, folk and world music is a growth area in touring for ICM who represent some of the biggest names in the field in the United States and worldwide, Mariachi Los Camperos de Nati Cano, Sweet Honey In The Rock, and Ravi and Anoushka Shankar.

Line-Up pmc

9a Tankerville Place
Newcastle upon Tyne NE2 3AT
T: 44 (0) 191 281 6449
F: 44 (0) 191 212 0913
E: chrismurtagh@line-up.co.uk
W: www.on-line-records.co.uk
C: Chris Murtagh

Line-Up pmc was established in 1978 by Chris Murtagh. It is a promotions and marketing consultancy dealing with live performance arts, entertainment, sporting and open-air events, incorporating event planning and management, artist management and representation.

Mintaka Management

Woodmans
Pishill
Henley-on-Thames
Oxon RG9 6HJ
T: 44 (0) 1491 639439
F: 44 (0) 1491 639539
E: glawson@worldmusicnet.net
W: www.worldmusicnet.net
C: Graham Lawson

Graham and Janine Lawson own and run Mintaka Management. Graham started in the music business in the early 1970s and has 25 years experience on 'both sides of the fence' as a record company MD, promoter and artist manager. Their ethos is: 'The artists have a vision and we help them realise it.' Mintaka concentrates on career development and has arranged the worldwide recording, publishing, sponsorship and live activities for its artists, which include Stomu Yamash'ta, Klaus Schulze, Gong, Huun Huur Tu and Trilok Gurtu.

The Nazareth Orchestra, soloist
Lubna Salame on stage with the
London Sinfonietta, conductor Martyn
Brabbins and Thom Yorke of Radiohead
at the Ether Festival, Royal Festival Hall
Photo: Justin Piperger

Moneypenny
The Stables
Westwood House
Main Street
North Dalton
East Yorkshire YO25 9XA
T: 44 (0) 1377 217815
F: 44 (0) 1377 217754
E: nigel@adastra-music.co.uk
W: www.adastra-music.co.uk/moneypenny
C: Nigel Morton

Moneypenny is a well-established stand-alone booking agency with a wealth of knowledge across the folk and world music scene. They work with a variety of acts covering a wide variety of styles, genres and nationalities – classic rock, world music, folk, singer-songwriters and progressive rock. The agency represents acts both nationally and internationally and books tours for its clients in venues as wide-ranging as small civic halls through to national concert halls, and major internationally recognised festivals, in addition to working with some of the leading UK and European promoters.

Musicians Incorporated
45 Harcourt Road
Alexandra Palace
London N22 7XW
T: 44 (0) 20 8888 1064
F: 44 (0) 20 8888 1026
E: info@musiciansincorporated.com
W: www.musiciansincorporated.com
C: Jason Walsh

Agent and booker for music acts from around the world including Orchestra Baobab, Daara J, Khaled, Femi Kuti, Souad Massi, The Skatalites, The Wailers, Rachid Taha, Louie Vega and his Elements of Life.

SASA Music
309 Aberdeen House
22–24 Highbury Grove
London N5 2EA
T: 44 (0) 20 7359 9232
F: 44 (0) 20 7359 9233
E: rab@sasa.demon.co.uk
W: www.sasamusic.com
C: David Flower

SASA Music was established in 1989 in London and since then has arranged, with its network of partners abroad, about 100 tours in Europe and beyond, as well as other singular events, for a wide selection of international music artists from Buena Vista Social Club from Cuba to Lo'jo from France, to Manecas Costa from Guinea Bissau and Tinariwen from Mali. SASA Music is also involved with the management of some of these artists, arranging recording contracts and publishing deals.

Serious
Chapel House
18 Hatton Place
London EC1N 8RU
T: 44 (0) 20 7405 9900
F: 44 (0) 20 7405 9911
E: info@serious.org.uk
W: www.serious.org.uk

Serious work with a wide range of musicians and composers from all over the world and create collaborations and commissions. Their projects range from large festivals to intimate clubs and from international tours to specially commissioned major events. They also have a commitment to audience and artist development, education work at all levels and music publishing. Serious acts as worldwide management for a range of major international artists on tour around the UK. These include composer/performers Taraf de Haidouks and world music artists as varied as Ladysmith Black Mambazo, Paco De Lucia, Chick Corea and Hugh Masekela. (See also Serious in Venues and promoters: London.)

Tumi Music
8/9 New Bond Street Place
Bath BA1 1BH
T: 44 (0) 1225 464736
F: 44 (0) 1225 444870
E: info@tumimusic.com
W: www.tumimusic.com

Tumi Music run a management side for artists on their own label Tumi (see their main entry in Labels and distributors).

YaD Arts
(See Venues and promoters.)

Labels and distributors

ARC Music Productions Int Ltd
PO Box 111
East Grinstead
West Sussex RH19 4FZ
T: 44 (0) 1342 328567
F: 44 (0) 1342 315958
E: info@arcmusic.co.uk
W: www.arcmusic.co.uk

Arc has a large catalogue of world music of over 410 recordings (over 50 releases each year) of African, Arabian, Asian, Celtic, Spanish, Gypsy, Latin American. Key artists include Egypt's 'ambassador of rhythm' Hossam Ramzy and the UK's Jewish ensemble The Burning Bush.

Cloud Valley Music
51 Hainault Court
Forest Rise
London E17 3NW
T: 44 (0) 20 8521 4649
E: cloudval@aol.com
W: members.aol.com/cloudval
C: Andrew Cronshaw

Cloud Valley is English composer and multi-instrumentalist Andrew Cronshaw's own label and home to his album *Ochre*, which was nominated on the shortlist of four CDs for the *fRoots* Critics Award in the 2005 BBC Radio 3 Awards for World Music.

Cooking Vinyl
PO Box 1845
London W3 0ZA
T: 44 (0) 20 8600 9200
F: 44 (0) 20 8743 7448
E: info@cookingvinyl.com
W: www.cookingvinyl.com
C: Martin Goldschmidt

Formed in 1986 Cooking Vinyl has an eclectic roots-based roster with an inclusive policy when it comes to genre. It covers Americana, indie, folk, rock, blues and world music such as Sweet Honey In the Rock, the Bhundu Boys, SE Rogie, Doug Kershaw and world music compilations.

Yat-Kha's Albert Kuvez,
toured by CMN and Coda
Photo: Vasily Krivdik

The Dune Music Company Ltd
1st Floor
73 Canning Road
Harrow
Middlesex HA3 7SP
T: 44 (0) 20 8424 2807
F: 44 (0) 20 8861 5371
E: info@dune-music.com
W: www.dune-music.com
E: jazz@tomorrowswarriors.org.uk
W: www.tomorrowswarriors.org

Established in 1997, Dune Records is a British independent label and artist management company, which specialises in jazz and jazz-crossover music. It has a number of award-winning artists and critically acclaimed albums to its name. It represents a growing number of Black artists and Black-led groups who work in an international, multicultural context and are keen to take jazz to a wider audience, by incorporating rap, hip hop, R&B, and reggae into their music. Artists include Soweto Kinch and Denys Baptiste. They also run an artist development and outreach programme through their sister company, Tomorrow's Warriors.

Afro Celt Sound System
on Real World Records
Photo: Kevin Westenberg

EMI Music
EMI House
43 Brook Green
London W6 7EF
T: 44 (0) 20 7605 5000
E: guy.hayden@emimusic.com
W: www.emigroup.com
C: Guy Hayden

EMI represent several labels in the UK that deal with world music releases, including Real World, Honest Jon's and On-U Sounds. They also represent artists signed to EMI companies around the world as well as several other labels internationally, including Narada who are based in the USA. EMI are the biggest independent label in the UK and while they are happy to receive music from artists and labels, they are not a distribution company and do not provide distribution for copies of finished albums.

Far Side Music
(See Agents and managers.)

Harmonia Mundi UK
45 Vyner Street
London E2 9DQ
T: 44 (0) 20 8709 9509
E: info.uk@harmoniamundi.com
W: www.harmoniamundi.com
C: Simon Astridge

Harmonia Mundi UK, the British branch of the multinational French record company and distributor, opened its London office in 1981. From the beginning it included a roster of jazz and world artists and labels among its specialist classical output.

Honest Jon's

278 Portobello Road
London W10 5TE
T: 44 (0) 20 8969 9822
F: 44 (0) 20 8969 5395
E: mail@honestjons.com
W: www.honestjons.com

Honest Jon's has been a London shop for 30 years. Now in collaboration with Damon Albarn, the expertise and knowledge behind this heritage has been extended into a record label. 'Honest Jon's is about bringing different cultures together in a natural way…wherever it comes from, if it's got the right attitude, it'll fit on the label,' said Albarn in an *Arena* magazine interview.

Nation Records

19 All Saints Road
London W11 1HE
T: 44 (0) 20 7792 8167
F: 44 (0) 20 7792 2854
E: akination@btopenworld.com
W: www.nationrecs.demon.co.uk

Nation was the original home of the Asian Underground, a fusion of eastern (Asian) music with western club and dance which grew in popularity from the early 1990s. Artists who have recorded with Nation include Fun-da-mental, Asian Dub Foundation, Loop Guru, Natacha Atlas and Transglobal Underground.

Navras Records

22 Sherwood Road
London NW4 1AD
T: 44 (0) 20 8203 2553
F: 44 (0) 20 8203 2542
E: music@navrasrecords.com
W: www.navrasrecords.com

Navras Records has one of the largest and most diverse catalogues of classical and traditional music from the Indian subcontinent, comprising some 230 titles. The catalogue is divided into sub-genres, such as Instrumental, Vocal, Duets (Jugalbandi), Light Classical (thumris and ghazals), Devotional (Sufi Qawwalis), Thematic, Folk, Fusion, etc. In addition to CD titles, Navras also carries DVD and CD-Rom software titles on its catalogue. The Navras catalogue incorporates virtually all the great maestros of the classical music genre from the subcontinent and specifically features an exclusive selection of the legendary sitar maestro, the late Ustad Vilayat Khan. Over 4/5ths of the catalogue features live recordings – a major raison d'être behind setting up of this label. The fusion/crossover titles on the Navras catalogue typically incorporates Indian classical with Jazz music – a natural compatibility in that both genres are improvisation oriented. Navras also promotes upcoming artists, through live concert recordings or studio recordings of classical or thematic/crossover material.

Proper Music Distribution

The New Powerhouse
Gateway Business Centre
Kangley Bridge Road
London SE26 5AN
T: 44 (0) 20 8676 5186
F: 44 (0) 20 9676 5190
E: properinfo@proper.uk.com
W: www.propermusic.com

The largest independent distributor in the UK with an extensive roster of world and roots labels from around the world.

Real World Records

Mill Lane
Box
Corsham SN13 8PL
T: 44 (0) 1225 743188
E: amanda.jones@realworld.co.uk
W: www.realworldrecords.com
C: Amanda Jones, Label Manager

Real World Records was founded in 1989 by WOMAD (see Festivals: South East) and Peter Gabriel to provide talented artists from around the world with access to state-of-the-art recording facilities and audiences beyond their geographical region. Consequently, the Real World label has become renowned for bringing together musicians who share an empathy with music in general, rather than a shared cultural background. Real World Records has grown into a label of wide-ranging, world-class music from all corners of the globe.

Sense World Music

93 Belgrave Road
Leicester LE4 6AS
T: 44 (0) 116 2667046
F: 44 (0) 116 2610480
E: info@senseworldmusic.com
W: www.senseworldmusic.com

Sense was founded in 1996 in order to bring together the many great talents from the global music community. Initially the company concentrated on Indian classical music and are now venturing into the Sufi-influenced music of Rajasthan. Their philosophy is simple, to produce the highest quality product with deep artistic consideration. They have studios near Anand in the North India countryside – 'Virtual Studios' is the first of its kind in India. It is a unique place for maintaining and developing the connection between nature, music and spirit. They also have a high quality, mobile multi-track location facility both in India and the UK, which is used at various live concerts and festivals. All recordings released by Sense are mixed and mastered in the UK.

Stern's Music

74/75 Warren Street
London W1T 5PF
T: 44 (0) 20 7387 5550
F: 44 (0) 20 7388 2756
E: info@sternsmusic.com
W: www.sternsmusic.com

Stern's was established in London in 1983 and specialises in African music. They have grown into the largest distributor of African records outside Paris, with a catalogue of 3,000 titles, including over a 100 on their own labels, Stern's and Earthworks.

Topic Records

50 Stroud Green Road
Finsbury Park
London N4 3ES
T: 44 (0) 20 7263 1240
F: 44 (0) 20 7281 5671
E: info@topicrecords.co.uk
W: www.topicrecords.co.uk

Independent London-based record label Topic Records has its roots in the Workers Music Association and can be traced back to 1939. The label remains dedicated to folk and world music. Its world music series includes a rich catalogue of compilations of music from all over the world including releases made in conjunction with the British Library Sound Archive (see Statutory agencies).

Triple Earth Records

7 Bullwood Road
Dunoon
Argyll PA23 7QJ
T: 44 (0) 1369 705886
E: iain@triple-earth.co.uk
W: www.triple-earth.co.uk
C: Iain Scott, Director

Established in 1983, Triple Earth has recently relocated to Scotland. Their back catalogue includes Najma Akhtar, Aster Aweke, Mose 'Fan Fan', Fuji Dub, Mouth Music and Hukwe Zawose. Their ears are always open, they say. Consultancy and production available.

Tumi Productions

8/9 New Bond Street Place
Bath BA1 1BH
T: 44 (0) 1225 446736
F: 44 (0) 1225 444870
E: info@tumimusic.com
W: www.tumimusic.com

(See also Agents and managers.) Founded in Bath in 1983 with the release of *City of Stone* by the Bolivian group Rumillajta, Tumi Productions has built its reputation on active artist promotion, encouraging a large touring network and providing a long-term commitment to artist development. Tumi has a solid catalogue of recordings by some of the best artists in Latin America and the Caribbean. The label has also experimented with 'cross-border' projects, like the award-nominated Banacongo collaboration between Papa Noel from Congo and Papi Oviedo from Cuba.

Union Square Music

Unit 1.1
Shepherds Studios
Rockley Road
London W14 0DA
T: 44 (0) 20 7471 7940
F: 44 (0) 20 7471 7941
E: info@unionsquaremusic.co.uk
W: www.unionsquaremusic.co.uk

Union Square has an extensive world music catalogue including compilation titles from all over the world and its colourful 'Café' series. It also produces the BBC Radio 3 World Music Awards CD, which contains tracks from all the nominated musicians and winners of the BBC Radio 3 Awards, and individual artist titles from Amelia Rodrigues, Khaled, Augustus Pablo and Manu Dibango and more.

World Circuit Records
1st Floor
Shoreditch Stables
138 Kingsland Road
London E2 8DY
T: 44 (0) 20 7749 3222
F: 44 (0) 20 7749 3232
E: info@worldcircuit.co.uk
W: www.worldcircuit.co.uk
C: Nick Gold, Director

World Circuit Records have established their reputation by producing some of the finest world music albums of the past two decades, specialising in music from Cuba and West Africa. The label is best known for the GRAMMY winning *Buena Vista Social Club* album (1997), which is the biggest-selling world music album of all time, and led to the phenomenal rise in the popularity of Cuban music. The *Buena Vista* series continues with solo albums from the GRAMMY winning Ibrahim Ferrer, Omara Portuondo, Cachaíto López, Rubén González, Guajiro Mirabal, and the innovative new album from Angá Díaz.

World Circuit's African artists enjoy equal prestige. Ali Farka Touré's GRAMMY winning *Talking Timbuktu* album (1994) recorded with Ry Cooder brought the label international acclaim, while other World Circuit artists such as Malian diva Oumou Sangare, the legendary Orchestra Baobab and musical maverick Cheikh Lô from Senegal have all emerged as major stars at home in Africa and around the globe. With their latest pairing of kora virtuoso Toumani Diabaté and Ali Farka Touré, World Circuit continues to set a high standard. No signings have come from unsolicited demos.

Buena Vista Social Club
on stage
Photo: Geraint Lewis

World Music Network/Riverboat Records

World Music Network
6 Abbeville Mews
88 Clapham Park Road
London SW4 7BX
T: 44 (0) 20 7498 5252
F: 44 (0) 20 7498 5353.
E: post@worldmusic.net
W: www.worldmusic.net

Founded in 1994 by Phil Stanton and Sandra Alayón-Stanton, World Music Network's albums are now distributed throughout 35 countries across the world. World Music Network makes the successful Rough Guide CDs, in association with the Rough Guide travel books (see Media: Books and reference guides). There are now over 150 Rough Guide albums covering countries as diverse as the Sahara, Bolivia Japan, Australia, Greece and Wales, and styles such as bellydance, South African gospel, gypsy swing, delta blues and bollywood. Music from the Rough Guide series can be heard on the online Rough Guide Radio Show (www.worldmusic.net/listen/radio.html). On Riverboat Records, World Music Network produces well-known world music artists such as Mory Kanté, Emmanuel Jal, Sierra Maestra, Bob Brozman and René Lacaille, and on the Introducing label, they produce lesser-known talents, such as Shiyani Ngcobo and Daby Baldé, who deserve to be brought into the spotlight.

Wrasse Records

Wrasse House
The Drive
Tyrrells Wood
Leatherhead KT22 8QW
T: 44 (0) 1372 376266
E: ian.ashbridge@wrasserecords.com
W: www.wrasserecords.com
C: Ian Ashbridge

Wrasse Records was established in 1997. The one criterion for music on Wrasse is that they 'must love it'. Wrasse sign albums from many sources – individuals, small companies and majors – and release these in every major territory around the world. The label works closely with agents and management to encourage and support live dates, as this is key to exposing the music to a wider audience. Their role is to expose the music to as many people as possible: to maximise exposure and therefore sales for all their artists. Artists include Ladysmith Black Mambazo, Lucky Dube, Angelique Kidjo, Ismael Lo, Salif keita, King Sunny Ade, Tinariwen and Pink Martini.